Goa

David Stott

Credits

Footprint credits
Editor: Nicola Gibbs
Production and layout: Emma Bryers
Maps: Kevin Feeney

Managing Director: Andy Riddle
Commercial Director: Patrick Dawson
Publisher: Alan Murphy
Publishing Managers: Felicity Laughton, Nicola Gibbs
Digital Editors: Jo Williams, Tom Mellors
Marketing and PR: Liz Harper
Sales: Diane McEntee
Advertising: Renu Sibal
Finance and Administration: Elizabeth Taylor

Photography credits
Front cover: Rafal Gaweda / Shutterstock
Back cover: Aleksandar Todorovic / Shutterstock

Printed in Great Britain by CPI Antony Rowe, Chippenham, Wiltshire

MIX
Paper from responsible sources
FSC
www.fsc.org
FSC® C013604

Every effort has been made to ensure that the facts in this guidebook are accurate. However, travellers should still obtain advice from consulates, airlines, etc about travel and visa requirements before travelling. The authors and publishers cannot accept responsibility for any loss, injury or inconvenience however caused.

Publishing information
Footprint *Focus Goa*
1st edition
© Footprint Handbooks Ltd
September 2011

ISBN: 978 1 908206 37 4
CIP DATA: A catalogue record for this book is available from the British Library

® Footprint Handbooks and the Footprint mark are a registered trademark of Footprint Handbooks Ltd

Published by Footprint
6 Riverside Court
Lower Bristol Road
Bath BA2 3DZ, UK
T +44 (0)1225 469141
F +44 (0)1225 469461
www.footprinttravelguides.com

Distributed in the USA by Globe Pequot Press, Guilford, Connecticut

The content of Footprint *Focus Goa* has been taken directly from Footprint's *India Handbook*, which was researched and written by David Stott, Vanessa Betts and Victoria McCulloch.

Contents

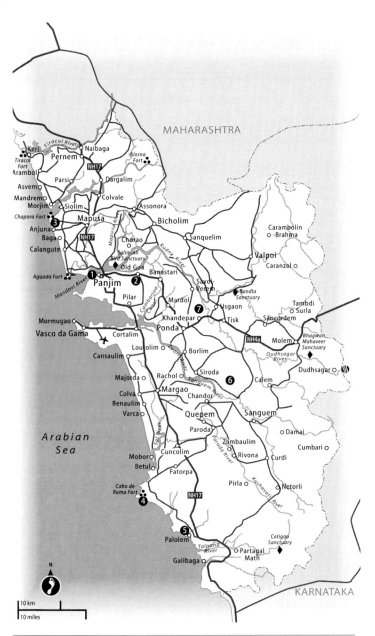

Goa, like San Francisco, Kathmandu and Spain, became a mecca for alternative living in the 1960s. Nowadays, it doesn't take much searching to find Costa Brava beer bellies and big-screen soccer intruding among the California tie-dye and palm-hung prayer flags, but if you don't need your sand Mr Whippy-white this tiny tranche of land remains, in pockets, unmatched. In most places you'll find little more than drowsy one-storey guesthouses strung along the beach, and away from the St George crosses and Kashmiri carpet shops the heartbeats of Goa's multilayered culture still pump good and strong: fishermen's boats rest on the sand beside sun loungers, Portuguese *fados* drift on the air in colonial villages, and the feral trance crew still hold their own at Anjuna's thrumming Saturday night market.

The relics of Goa's colonial past, though no match for the giant landmarks of broader India, are still rococo and baroque gems, half swallowed up by nature. Lush jungles twist their way around ruined forts, and huge banyans shelter centuries-old church spires and lavish basilicas.

There is humble everyday beauty to be had elsewhere too. At dawn in the villages, blue mists lie low and hazy across paddy fields and curl at the crumbling fronts of 18th-century Portuguese manors in pink, umber and blue. Exotic birds dive about sprawling raintrees and ravens caw as delivery boys push bicycles stacked with freshly baked breads. At sunset, the amber hues blaze against the mottled green Arabian Sea, fire embers smoke at the feet of chickens and pigs, bullock carts dredge through muddy fields of paddy and boys in board shorts swing their cricket bats in the straw stubble. Then at velvet twilight Goa's fisherfolk steal out of quiet harbours in brightly coloured trawlers, whose torches twinkle like a thread of fairy lights along the night horizon as they fill their nets with silvery pomfret and snapper. These gentle-paced and easy-living people also enjoy a shared flair for food, wine and song.

Planning your trip

When to go

Goa is always warm, but its coastal position means it never becomes unbearably hot. Nonetheless, from mid-April until the beginning of the monsoon in mid-June, both the temperature and humidity rise sharply, making for steamy hot days and balmy nights. The six weeks of the monsoon in June/July often come as torrential storms, while the warm dry weather of its tropical winter (October-March) is the best time to visit. Weather patterns are fluctuating: 2007 had the coldest January in 40 years; 2008 the hottest February for 40 years.

Getting there

Air

India is accessible by air from virtually every continent. Most international flights arrive in Delhi, Mumbai, Chennai or Kolkata. There are also international airports in several other cities (eg Ahmedabad, Bengaluru (Bangalore), Hyderabad, Thiruvananthapuram, Goa), some of which allow customs formalities to be completed there although the flight may be routed through a principal airport. Some carriers permit 'open-jaw' travel, arriving in, and departing from, different cities in India. Some (eg **Air India, British Airways**) have convenient non-stop flights from Europe, eg from London to Delhi, takes only nine hours.

Alternatively, you can fly to numerous destinations across India with **Jet Airways** or **Kingfisher**. The prices are very competitive if domestic flights are booked in conjunction with Jet on the international legs. In 2011 the cheapest return flights to Delhi from London started from around £400, but leapt to £800+ as you approached the high season of Christmas, New Year and Easter.

From Europe Despite the increases to Air Passenger Duty, Britain remains the cheapest place in Europe for flights to India. **Virgin Atlantic, British Airways** and **Kingfisher** fly from London to Delhi in 8½ hours or Mumbai in 9½ hours. From mainland Europe, **Jet Airways** flies to India from Brussels and Milan, while major European flag carriers including KLM and **Lufthansa** fly to Delhi and/or Mumbai from their respective hub airports. In most cases the cheapest flights are with Middle Eastern or Central Asian airlines, transiting via airports in the Gulf. Several airlines from the Middle East (eg **Emirates, Gulf Air, Kuwait Airways, Royal Jordanian, Qatar Airways, Oman Air**) offer good discounts to Mumbai and other Indian regional capitals from London, but fly via their hub cities, adding to the journey time. Consolidators in the UK can quote some competitive fares, such as: Flightbookers, T0871-223 5000, www.ebookers.com; **North South Travel**, T01245-608291, www.northsouthtravel.co.uk (profits to charity).

From North America From the east coast, several airlines including **Air India, Jet Airways, Continental** and **Delta** fly direct from New York to Delhi and Mumbai. **American** flies to both cities from Chicago. Discounted tickets on **British Airways, KLM, Lufthansa, Gulf Air** and **Kuwait Airways** are sold through agents although they will invariably fly via their

Don't miss ...

Numbers refer to the map on page 4.

country's capital cities. From the west coast, **Air India** flies from Los Angeles to Delhi and Mumbai, and **Jet Airways** from San Francisco to Mumbai via Shanghai. Alternatively, fly via Hong Kong, Singapore or Bangkok using one of those countries' national carriers. **Air Canada** operates between Vancouver and Delhi. **Air Brokers International**, www.airbrokers.com, is competitive and reputable. STA, www.statravel.co.uk, has offices in many US cities, Toronto and Ontario. Student fares are also available from **Travel Cuts**, www.travelcuts.com, in Canada.

From Australasia Qantas, Singapore Airlines, Thai Airways, Malaysian Airlines, Cathay Pacific and Air India are the principal airlines connecting the continents, although Qantas is the only one that flies direct, with services from Sydney to Mumbai. **Tiger Airways** run a no-frills service from Darwin to Kochi via Singapore, and **Air Asia X** operates from Melbourne and the Gold Coast to several South Indian cities via Kuala Lumpur; these flights can be much cheaper than standard airlines, at the cost of extended layovers and the usual extra charges for checked luggage, food, etc. STA and **Flight Centre** offer discounted tickets from their branches in major cities in Australia and New Zealand. **Abercrombie & Kent**, www.abercrombiekent.co.uk, **Adventure World**, www.adventure world.net.au, **Peregrine**, www.peregrineadventures.com, and **Travel Corporation of India**, www.tcindia.com, organize tours.

Airport information The formalities on arrival in India have been increasingly streamlined during the last few years and the facilities at the major international airports greatly improved. However, arrival can still be a slow process. Disembarkation cards, with an attached customs declaration, are handed out to passengers during the inward flight. The immigration form should be handed in at the immigration counter on arrival. The customs slip will be returned, for handing over to the customs on leaving the baggage collection hall. You may well find that there are delays of over an hour at immigration in processing passengers passing through immigration who need help with filling in forms.

   Departure tax Rs 500 is payable for all international departures other than those to neighbouring SAARC countries, when the tax is Rs 250 (not reciprocated by Sri Lanka). This is normally included in your international ticket; check when buying. (To save time 'Security Check' your baggage before checking in at departure.)

Getting around

Air

India has a comprehensive network linking the major cities of the different states. Deregulation of the airline industry has had a transformative effect on travel within India, with a host of low-budget private carriers offering sometimes unbelievably cheap fares on an ever-expanding network of routes in a bid to woo the train-travelling middle class. Promotional fares as low as Rs 9 (US$0.20) are not unknown, though such numbers are rendered somewhat meaningless by additional taxes and fuel charges – an extra US$30-50 on most flights. On any given day, booking a few days in advance, you can expect to fly between Delhi and Mumbai for around US$100 one way including taxes, while a month's notice and flying with a no-frills airline can reduce the price to US$70-80; regional routes, eg Mumbai–Kozhikode in north Kerala, are often cheaper than routes between main cities.

Competition from the efficiently run private sector has, in general, improved the quality of services provided by the nationalized airlines. It also seems to herald the end of the two-tier pricing structure, meaning that ticket prices are now usually the same for foreign and Indian travellers. The airport authorities too have made efforts to improve handling on the ground.

Although flying is comparatively expensive, for covering vast distances or awkward links on a route it is an option worth considering, though delays and re-routing can be irritating. For short distances, and on some routes (eg Delhi–Agra–Delhi), it makes more sense to travel by train. If you don't want to take a connecting flight down to Goa, the Konkan railway makes a pretty, and increasingly speedy, alternative. Don't be tempted to take the bus.

The best way to get an idea of the current routes, carriers and fares is to use a third-party booking website such as www.cheapairticketsindia.com (toll-free numbers: UK T0800-101 0928, USA T1-888 825 8680), www.cleartrip.com, www.makemytrip.co.in, or www.yatra.com. Booking with these is a different matter: some refuse foreign credit cards outright, while others have to be persuaded to give your card special clearance. Tickets booked on these sites are typically issued as an email ticket or an SMS text message – the simplest option if you have an Indian mobile phone, though it must be converted to a paper ticket at the relevant carrier's airport offices before you will be allowed into the terminal. Makemytrip.com and Travelocity.com both accept international credit cards.

Rail

Trains can still be the cheapest and most comfortable means of travelling long distances saving you hotel expenses on overnight journeys. It gives access to booking station Retiring Rooms, which can be useful from time to time. Above all, you have an ideal opportunity to meet local travellers and catch a glimpse of life on the ground. Remember the dark glass on air-conditioned coaches does restrict vision. See also www.indianrail.gov.in.

High-speed trains There are several air-conditioned 'high-speed' **Shatabdi** (or 'Century') **Express** for day travel, and **Rajdhani Express** ('Capital City') for overnight journeys. These cover large sections of the network but due to high demand you need to book them well in advance (up to 90 days). Meals and drinks are usually included.

Royal trains You can travel like a maharaja on the **Palace on Wheels** (www.palaceon wheels.net), the famous seven-nighter which has been running for many years and gives visitors an opportunity to see some of the 'royal' cities in Rajasthan during the winter

Goa ins and outs

Vasco da Gama is the passenger railway terminus of the Central Goa branch line, and is the capital of the industrial heart of modern Goa. Dabolim Airport is 3 km away and was developed by the Navy. It is currently shared between the needs of the military and the escalating demands of tourism. Vasco is 30 km from Panjim, the main arrival point for long-distance buses. Trains via Londa bring visitors from the north and east (Delhi and Agra, Hospet and Bengaluru) while trains from Mumbai, Kerala and coastal points in between arrive via the Konkan Railway, which offers several jumping-off points in Goa besides the main station at Margao (Madgaon). For rail reservations, call T0832-251 2833.

Charter companies fly direct to Dabolim Airport between October and April from the UK, the Netherlands, Switzerland and Russia. There are several flights daily from various cities in India (including Mumbai, Thiruvananthapuram, Bengaluru, Delhi and Chennai) with Air India, Indian Airlines, Kingfisher and Jet Airways.

Package tour companies and luxury hotels usually arrange courtesy buses for hotel transfer, but even if you're coming independently the Arrivals terminal is relatively relaxed. A pre-paid taxi counter immediately outside has rates clearly displayed (such as Panjim Rs 450, 40 minutes; north Goa beaches from Rs 700; Tiracol Rs 1400; Arambol Rs 1200; south Goa beaches from Rs 500; Palolem Rs 900). State your destination at the counter, pay and obtain a receipt that will give the registration number of your taxi. Keep hold of this receipt until you reach your destination. The public bus stop on the far side of the roundabout outside the airport gates has buses to Vasco da Gama, from where there are connections to all the major destinations in Goa.

A popular way to get around is by hiring a scooter, available in all towns and villages. However, make sure the bike has yellow and black number plates, which signal that the vehicle is for hire; plain black-and-white plates could result in a fine from the police.

months for around US$2500. A wonderful way to travel but time at the destinations is a little compressed for some. Two other seven-nighters are the **Deccan Odyssey** (www.indiarail.co.uk/do.htm), a train running in Maharashtra, and the **Golden Chariot** (www.indiarail.co.uk/gt.htm), a relatively new option running in Karnataka covering Belur, Halebid, Shravanabelagola and then Hampi and Badami/Aihole/Pattadakal. The **Heritage on Wheels** (www.heritageonwheels.org.in), a meter-gauge train covering the Shekawati region, Tal Chappar and Bikaner, starts and concludes in Jaipur. Bookings and more information for all these heritage-style trains is available at www.indrail.co.uk.
Steam For rail enthusiasts, the steam-hauled narrow-gauge trains between Kurseong and Darjeeling in North Bengal (a World Heritage Site), and between Mettupalayam and Coonoor, and a special one between Ooty and Runnymede in the Nilgiris, are an attraction. See the IRCTC and Indian Railways website, www.irctc.co.in. **Williams Travel**, 18/20 Howard St, Belfast BT1 6FQ, Northern Ireland, T028-9023 0714, www.williams-travel.co.uk, and **SDEL** (see page 11) are recommended for tailor-made trips.

Train touts

Many railway stations – and some bus stations and major tourist sites – are heavily populated with touts. Self-styled 'agents' will board trains before they enter the station and seek out tourists, often picking up their luggage and setting off with words such as "Madam!/Sir! Come with me madam/sir! You need top-class hotel …". They will even select porters to take your luggage without giving you any say.

If you have succeeded in getting off the train or even in obtaining a trolley you will find hands eager to push it for you.

For a first-time visitor such touts can be more than a nuisance. You need to keep calm and firm. Decide in advance where you want to stay. If you need a porter on trains, select one yourself and agree a price **before** the porter sets off with your baggage. If travelling with a companion one can stay guarding the luggage while the other gets hold of a taxi and negotiates the price to the hotel. It sounds complicated and sometimes it feels it. The most important thing is to behave as if you know what you are doing!

Classes **A/c First Class**, available only on main routes, is very comfortable (bedding provided). It will also be possible for tourists to reserve special coaches (some air conditioning) which are normally allocated to senior railway officials only. **A/c Sleeper**, two and three-tier configurations (known as 2AC and 3AC), are clean and comfortable and popular with middle class families; these are the safest carriages for women travelling alone. **A/c Executive Class**, with wide reclining seats, are available on many Shatabdi trains at double the price of the ordinary **a/c Chair Car** which are equally comfortable. **First Class (non-a/c)** is gradually being phased out, and is now restricted to a handful of routes in the south, but the run-down old carriages still provide a pleasant experience if you like open windows. **Second Class (non-a/c)** two and three-tier (commonly called **Sleeper**), provides exceptionally cheap and atmospheric travel, with basic padded vinyl seats and open windows that allow the sights and sounds of India (not to mention dust, insects and flecks of spittle expelled by passengers up front) to drift into the carriage. On long journeys Sleeper can be crowded and uncomfortable, and toilet facilities can be unpleasant; it is nearly always better to use the Indian-style squat loos rather than the Western-style ones as they are better maintained. At the bottom rung is **Unreserved Second Class**, with hard wooden benches. You can travel long distances for a trivial amount of money, but unreserved carriages are often ridiculously crowded, and getting off at your station may involve a battle of will and strength against the hordes trying to shove their way on.

Indrail passes These allow travel across the network without having to pay extra reservation fees and sleeper charges but you have to spend a high proportion of your time on the train to make it worthwhile. However, the advantages of pre-arranged reservations and automatic access to 'Tourist Quotas' can tip the balance in favour of the pass for some travellers.

Tourists (foreigners and Indians resident abroad) may buy these passes from the tourist sections of principal railway booking offices and pay in foreign currency, major credit cards, travellers' cheques or rupees with encashment certificates. Fares range from US$57 to US$1060 for adults or half that for children. Rail-cum-air tickets are also to be made available.

Indrail passes can also conveniently be bought abroad from special agents. For people contemplating a single long journey soon after arriving in India, the Half- or One-day Pass with a confirmed reservation is worth the peace of mind; two- or four-day passes are also sold.

The UK agent is **SDEL**, 103 Wembley Park Drive, Wembley, Middlesex HA9 8HG, UK, T020-8903 3411, www.indiarail.co.uk. They make all necessary reservations and offer excellent advice. They can also book Indian Airlines and Jet Airways internal flights.

A **White Pass** allows first class a/c travel (the top rung); a **Green**, a/c two-tier Sleepers and Chair Cars; and the **Yellow**, only second-class travel. Passes for up to four days' duration are only sold abroad.

Cost A/c first class costs about double the rate for two-tier shown below, and non a/c second class about half. Children (aged five to 12) travel at half the adult fare. The young (12-30 years) and senior citizens (65 years and over) are allowed a 30% discount on journeys over 500 km (just show your passport).

Period	US$ A/c 2-tier	Period	US$ A/c 2-tier
½ day	26	21 days	198
1 day	43	30 days	248
7 days	135	60 days	400
15 days	185	90 days	530

Fares for individual journeys are based on distance covered and reflect both the class and the type of train. Higher rates apply on the Mail and Express trains and the air-conditioned Shatabdi and Rajdhani Expresses.

Internet services Much information is available online via www.railtourismindia.com, www.indianrail.gov.in and www.trainenquiry.com, where you can check timetables (which change frequently), numbers, seat availability and even the running status of your train. Internet e-tickets can be bought and printed on www.irctc.in – a great time-saver when the system works properly. The credit card process can be complicated, and at time of writing is off-limits to credit cards issued outside India. The best option is to use a third-party agent such as www.makemytrip.com or www.cleartrip.com, which provide an easily-understood booking engine and accept foreign cards. An alternative is to seek a local agent who can sell e-tickets, which can cost as little as Rs 5-10 (plus Rs 20 reservation fee, some agents charge up to Rs 150 a ticket, however), and can save hours of hassle; simply present the printout to the ticket collector. However, it is tricky if you then want to cancel an e-ticket which an agent has bought for you on their account.

Note All train numbers changed to five-digit numbers in 2010-2011; in most cases, adding a '1' to the start of an old four-figure number will produce the new number. Otherwise, try your luck with the 'train number enquiry' search at www.indianrail.gov.in/inet_trnno_enq.html.

Tickets and reservations It is now possible to reserve tickets for virtually any train on the network from one of the 1000 computerized reservation centres across India. It is always best to book as far in advance as possible (usually up to 60 days). To reserve a seat on a particular train, note down the train's name, number and departure time and fill in a reservation form while you line up at the ticket window; you can use one form for up to four passengers. At busy stations the wait can take an hour or more. You can save a lot of time and effort by asking a travel agent to get your tickets for a fee of Rs 50-100. If the class you want is full, ask if special 'quotas' are available (see above). If not, consider buying a 'wait list' ticket, as seats often become available close to the train's departure time; phone the station on the day of departure to check your ticket's status. If you don't have a reservation for a particular train but carry an Indrail Pass, you may get one by arriving three hours early. Be wary of touts at the station offering tickets, hotels or exchange.

Timetables Regional timetables are available cheaply from station bookstalls; the monthly *Indian Bradshaw* is sold in principal stations. The handy *Trains at a Glance* (Rs 30) lists popular trains likely to be used by most foreign travellers and is available at stalls at Indian railway stations and in the UK from SDEL (see page 11).

Road

Road travel is often the only choice for reaching many of the places of outstanding interest in which India is so rich. For the uninitiated, travel by road can also be a worrying experience because of the apparent absence of conventional traffic regulations and also in the mountains, especially during the rainy season when landslides are possible. Vehicles drive on the left – in theory. Routes around the major cities are usually crowded with lorry traffic, especially at night, and the main roads are often poor and slow. There are a few motorway-style expressways, but most main roads are single track. Some district roads are quiet, and although they are not fast they can be a good way of seeing the country and village life if you have the time.

Bus Buses now reach virtually every part of India, offering a cheap, if often uncomfortable, means of visiting places off the rail network. Very few villages are now more than 2-3 km from a bus stop. Services are run by the State Corporation from the State Bus Stand (and private companies which often have offices nearby). The latter allow advance reservations, including booking printable e-tickets online (check www.redbus.in and www.viaworld.in) and, although tickets prices are a little higher, they have fewer stops and are a bit more comfortable. In the absence of trains, buses are often the only budget option, into the Himalaya for example. There are many sleeper buses (a contradiction in terms) running Mumbai–Goa or into the Himalaya – if you must take a sleeper bus, choose a lower berth near the front of the bus. The upper berths are almost always really uncomfortable.

Bus categories Though comfortable for sightseeing trips, apart from the very best 'sleeper coaches' even **air-conditioned luxury coaches** can be very uncomfortable for really long journeys. Often the air conditioning is very cold so wrap up. Journeys over 10 hours can be extremely tiring so it is better to go by train if there is a choice. **Express buses** run over long distances (frequently overnight), these are often called 'video coaches' and can be an appalling experience unless you appreciate loud film music blasting through the night. Ear plugs and eye masks may ease the pain. They rarely average more than 45 kph. **Local buses** are often very crowded, quite bumpy, slow and usually poorly maintained. However, over short distances, they can be a very cheap, friendly and easy way of getting about. Even where signboards are not in English someone will usually give you directions. Many larger towns have **minibus** services which charge a little more than the buses and pick up and drop passengers on request. Again very crowded, and with restricted headroom, they are the fastest way of getting about many of the larger towns.

Bus travel tips Some towns have different bus stations for different destinations. Booking on major long-distance routes is now computerized. Book in advance where possible and avoid the back of the bus where it can be very bumpy. If your destination is only served by a local bus you may do better to take the Express bus and 'persuade' the driver, with a tip in advance, to stop where you want to get off. You will have to pay the full fare to the first stop beyond your destination but you will get there faster and more comfortably. When an unreserved bus pulls into a bus station, there is usually an unholy scramble for seats, whilst those arriving have to struggle to get off! In many areas there is an unwritten 'rule of reservation' using handkerchiefs or bags thrust through the windows to reserve seats. Some visitors may feel a more justified right to a seat having fought their way through the crowd, but it is generally best to do as local people do and be prepared with a handkerchief or 'sarong'. As soon as it touches the seat, it is yours! Leave it on your seat when getting off to use the toilet at bus stations.

Car A car provides a chance to travel off the beaten track, and gives unrivalled opportunities for seeing something of India's great variety of villages and small towns. Until recently, the most widely used hire car was the Hindustan Ambassador. However, except for the newest model, they are often very unreliable, and although they still have their devotees, many find them uncomfortable for long journeys. For a similar price, Maruti cars and vans (Omni) are much more reliable and are now the preferred choice in many areas. Gypsy 4WDs and Jeeps are also available, especially in the hills, where larger Sumos have made an appearance. Maruti Esteems and Toyota Qualis are comfortable and have optional reliable air-conditioning. A specialist operator can be very helpful in arranging itineraries and car hire in advance.

Car hire With a driver, car hire is cheaper than in the West. A car shared by three or four can be very good value. Be sure to check carefully the mileage at the beginning and end of the trip. Two- or three-day trips from main towns can also give excellent opportunities for sightseeing off the beaten track in reasonable comfort. Local drivers often know their way much better than drivers from other states, so where possible it is a good idea to get a local driver who speaks the state language, in addition to being able to communicate with you. In the mountains, it is better to use a driver who knows the roads. Drivers may sleep in the car overnight although hotels (especially pricier ones) should provide a bed for them. They are responsible for their expenses, including meals. Car (and auto) drivers increase their earnings by taking you to hotels and shops where they get a handsome commission (which you will pay for). If you feel inclined, a tip at the end of the tour of Rs 100 per day in addition to their daily allowance is perfectly acceptable. Check beforehand if fuel and inter-state taxes are included in the hire charge.

Cars can be hired through private companies. International companies such as **Hertz**, **Europcar** and **Budget** operate in some major cities and offer reliable cars; their rates are generally higher than those of local firms (eg **Sai Service, Wheels**). The price of an imported car can be three times that of the Ambassador.

Car with driver	Economy Maruti 800 Ambassador	Regular a/c Maruti 800 Contessa	Premium a/c Maruti 1000 Opel	Luxury a/c Esteem Qualis
8 hrs/80 km	Rs 800	Rs 1000	Rs 1400	Rs 1800+
Extra km	Rs 4-7	Rs 9	Rs 13	Rs 18
Extra hour	Rs 40	Rs 50	Rs 70	Rs 100
Out of town				
Per km	Rs 7	Rs 9	Rs 13	Rs 18
Night halt	Rs 100	Rs 200	Rs 250	Rs 250

Taxi Yellow-top taxis in cities and large towns are metered, although tariffs change frequently. These changes are shown on a fare chart which should be read in conjunction with the meter reading. Increased night time rates apply in some cities, and there is a small charge for luggage. Insist on the taxi meter being flagged in your presence. If the driver refuses, the official advice is to contact the police. This may not work, but it is worth trying. When a taxi doesn't have a meter, you will need to fix the fare before starting the journey. Ask at your hotel desk for a guide price. As a foreigner, it is rare to get a taxi in the big cities to use the meter – if they are eager to, watch out as sometimes the meter is rigged and they have a fake rate card. Also, watch out for the David Blaine-style note shuffle: you pay with a Rs 500 note, but they have a Rs 100 note in their hand. This happens frequently at the pre-paid booth outside New Delhi train station too, no matter how small the transaction.

At stations and airports it is often possible to share taxis to a central point. It is worth looking for fellow passengers who may be travelling in your direction and get a pre-paid taxi. At night, always have a clear idea of where you want to go and insist on being taken there. Taxi drivers may try to convince you that the hotel you have chosen 'closed three years ago' or is 'completely full'. Say that you have a reservation.

Rickshaw **Auto-rickshaws** (autos) are almost universally available in towns across India and are the cheapest and most convenient way of getting about. It is best to walk a short distance away from a hotel gate before picking up an auto to avoid paying an inflated rate. In addition to using them for short journeys it is often possible to hire them by the hour, or for a half or full day's sightseeing. In some areas younger drivers who speak some English and know their local area well may want to show you around. However, rickshaw drivers are often paid a commission by hotels, restaurants and gift shops so advice is not always impartial. Drivers generally refuse to use a meter, often quote a ridiculous price or may sometimes stop short of your destination. If you have real problems it can help to note down the vehicle licence number and threaten to go to the police. Beware of some rickshaw drivers who show the fare chart for taxis, especially in Mumbai.

Cycle-rickshaws and **horse-drawn tongas** are more common in the more rustic setting of a small town or the outskirts of a large one. You will need to fix a price by bargaining. The animal attached to a tonga usually looks too undernourished to have the strength to pull the driver, let alone passengers.

Sleeping

India has an enormous range of accommodation. You can stay safely and very cheaply by Western standards right across the country. In all the major cities there are also high-quality hotels, offering a full range of facilities; in small centres hotels are much more variable. In Rajasthan and Gujarat, old Maharajas' palaces and forts have been privately converted into comfortable, unusual hotels. Hotels in beach resorts and hill stations, because of their location and special appeal, often deviate from the description of our different categories. In the peak season (October to April for most of India) bookings can be extremely heavy in popular destinations. It is sometimes possible to book in advance by phone, fax or email, but double check your reservation, and always try to arrive as early as possible in the day.

Hotels → *For Sleeping price codes, see box, page 16.*

Price categories The category codes used in this book are based on prices of double rooms excluding taxes. They are **not** star ratings and individual facilities vary considerably. The most expensive hotels charge in US dollars only. Modest hotels may not have their own restaurant but will often offer 'room service', bringing in food from outside. In South and West India, and in temple towns, restaurants may only serve vegetarian food. Many hotels operate a 24-hour checkout system. Make sure that this means that you can stay 24 hours from the time of check-in. Expect to pay more in Delhi, Mumbai and, to a lesser extent, in Bengaluru (Bangalore), Chennai and Kolkata for all categories; Kerala, too, is becoming quite expensive. Prices away from large cities tend to be lower for comparable hotels. Away from the metropolitan cities, in South India, room rates tend to be lower than the North, and the standard of cleanliness is higher.

Off-season rates Large reductions are made by hotels in all categories out-of-season in many resorts. Always ask if any is available. You may also request the 10-15% agent's commission to be deducted from your bill if you book direct. Clarify whether the agreed figure includes all taxes.

Taxes In general most hotel rooms rated at Rs 1200 or above are subject to a tax of 10%. Many states levy an additional luxury tax of 10-25%, and some hotels add a service charge of 10% on top of this. Taxes are not necessarily payable on meals, so it is worth settling your meals bill separately. Most hotels in the **$$** category and above accept payment by credit card. Check your final bill carefully. Visitors have complained of incorrect bills, even in the most expensive hotels. The problem particularly afflicts groups, when last-minute extras appear mysteriously on some guests' bills. Check the evening before departure, and keep all receipts.

Hotel facilities You have to be prepared for difficulties which are uncommon in the West. It is best to inspect the room and check that all equipment (air conditioning, TV, water heater, flush) works before checking in at a modest hotel. Many hotels try to wring too many years' service out of their linen, and it's quite common to find sheets that are stained, frayed or riddled with holes. Don't expect any but the most expensive or tourist-savvy hotels to fit a top sheet to the bed.

In some states **power cuts** are common, or hot water may be restricted to certain times of day. The largest hotels have their own generators but it is best to carry a good torch.

In some regions **water supply** is rationed periodically. Keep a bucket filled to use for flushing the toilet during water cuts. Occasionally, tap water may be discoloured due to

---

Sleeping and eating price codes

Sleeping

$$$$	over US$150	$$$	US$66-150
$$	US$30-65	$	under US$30

For a double room in high season, excluding taxes.

Eating

$$$	over US$12	$$	US$6-12	$	under US$6

For a two-course meal for one person, excluding drinks and service charge.

rusty tanks. During the cold weather and in hill stations, hot water will be available at certain times of the day, sometimes in buckets, but is usually very restricted in quantity. Electric water heaters may provide enough for a shower but not enough to fill a bath tub. For details on drinking water, see page 17.

Hotels close to temples can be very **noisy**, especially during festivals. Music blares from loudspeakers late at night and from very early in the morning, often making sleep impossible. Mosques call the faithful to prayers at dawn. Some find ear plugs helpful.

Homestays

At the upmarket end, increasing numbers of travellers are keen to stay in private homes and guesthouses, opting not to book large hotel chains that keep you at arm's length from a culture. Instead, travellers get home-cooked meals in heritage houses and learn about a country through conversation with often fascinating hosts. Kerala leads the way in this field, but Delhi is catching up fast, with dozens of new and smart family-run B&Bs springing up. Tourist offices have lists of families with more modest homestays. Companies specializing in homestays include **Kerala Connections**, www.keralaconnect. co.uk, **MAHout**, www.mahoutuk.com, **Pyramid Tours**, www.pyramidtravelindia.com and **Sundale Vacations**, www.sundale.com.

Eating and drinking → *For Eating price codes, see box, page 16.*

Food

You find just as much variety in dishes and presentation crossing South India as you would on an equivalent journey across Europe. Combinations of spices give each region its distinctive flavour.

The larger hotels, open to non-residents, often offer **buffet** lunches with Indian, Western and sometimes Chinese dishes. These can be good value (Rs 250-300; but Rs 450 in the top grades) and can provide a welcome, comfortable break in the cool. The health risks, however, of food kept warm for long periods in metal containers are considerable, especially if turnover at the buffet is slow. We have received several complaints of stomach trouble following a buffet meal, even in five-star hotels.

It is essential to be very careful since food hygiene may be poor, flies abound and refrigeration in the hot weather may be inadequate and intermittent because of power cuts. It is best to eat only freshly prepared food by ordering from the menu (especially meat and fish dishes). Avoid salads and cut fruit.

If you are unused to spicy food, go slow. Stick to Western or mild Chinese meals in good restaurants and try the odd Indian dish to test your reaction. Food is often spicier when you eat with families or at local places. Popular local restaurants are obvious from the number of people eating in them. Try a traditional *thali*, which is a complete meal served on a large stainless steel plate (or very occasionally on a banana leaf). Several preparations, placed in small bowls, surround the central serving of wholewheat chapati and rice. A vegetarian *thali* would include dhal (lentils), two or three curries (which can be quite hot) and crisp poppadums, although there are regional variations. A variety of pickles are offered – mango and lime are two of the most popular. These can be exceptionally hot, and are designed to be taken in minute quantities alongside the main dishes. Plain *dahi* (yoghurt) in the south, or *raita* in the north, usually acts as a bland 'cooler'. Simple *dhabas* (rustic roadside eateries) are an alternative experience for sampling authentic local dishes.

Many city restaurants offer a choice of so-called **European options** such as toasted sandwiches, stuffed pancakes, apple pies, fruit crumbles and cheesecakes. Italian favourites (pizzas, pastas) can be very different from what you are used to. In the big cities, Goa and Dharamshala, the Western food is generally pretty good. Western confectionery, in general, is disappointing. **Ice creams**, on the other hand, can be exceptionally good; there are excellent Indian ones as well as some international brands.

India has many delicious tropical **fruits**. Some are seasonal (eg mangoes, pineapples and lychees), while others (eg bananas, grapes and oranges) are available throughout the year. It is safe to eat the ones you can wash and peel.

Drink

Drinking water used to be regarded as one of India's biggest hazards. It is still true that water from the tap or a well should never be considered safe to drink since public water supplies are often polluted. Bottled water is now widely available although not all bottled water is mineral water; most are simply purified water from an urban supply. Buy from a shop or stall, check the seal carefully (some companies now add a second clear plastic seal around the bottle top) and avoid street hawkers; when disposing bottles puncture the neck which prevents misuse but allows recycling.

There is growing concern over the mountains of plastic bottles that are collecting and the waste of resources needed to produce them, so travellers are being encouraged to use alternative methods of getting safe drinking water. In some towns such as Dharamshala and Leh, purified water is now sold for refilling your own container. You may wish to purify water yourself. A portable water filter is a good idea, carrying the drinking water in a plastic bottle in an insulated carrier. Always carry enough drinking water with you when travelling. It is important to use pure water for cleaning teeth.

Tea and **coffee** are safe and widely available. Both are normally served sweet, and with milk. If you wish, say 'no sugar' (*chini nahin*), 'no milk' (*dudh nahin*) when ordering. Alternatively, ask for a pot of tea and milk and sugar to be brought separately. Freshly brewed coffee is a common drink in South India, but in the North, ordinary city restaurants will usually serve the instant variety. Even in aspiring smart cafés, espresso or cappuccino may not turn out quite as you'd expect in the West.

Bottled **soft drinks** such as Coke, Pepsi, Teem, Limca, Thums Up and Gold Spot are universally available but always check the seal when you buy from a street stall. There are also several brands of fruit juice sold in cartons, including mango, pineapple and apple – Indian brands are very sweet. Don't add ice cubes as the water source may be contaminated. Take care with fresh fruit juices or *lassis* as ice is often added.

Indians rarely drink **alcohol** with a meal. In the past wines and spirits were generally either imported and extremely expensive, or local and of poor quality. Now, the best Indian whisky, rum and brandy (IMFL or 'Indian Made Foreign Liquor') are widely accepted, as are good Champagnoise and other wines from Maharashtra. If you hanker after a bottle of imported wine, you will only find it in the top restaurants for at least Rs 800-1000.

For the urban elite, refreshing Indian beers are popular when eating out and so are widely available. 'Pubs' have sprung up in the major cities. Elsewhere, seedy, all-male drinking dens in the larger cities are best avoided for women travellers, but can make quite an experience otherwise – you will sometimes be locked into cubicles for clandestine drinking. If that sounds unsavoury then head for the better hotel bars instead; prices aren't that steep. In rural India, local rice, palm, cashew or date juice *toddy* and *arak* is deceptively potent. However, the Sikkimese *chhang* makes a pleasant change drunk out of a wooden tankard through a bamboo straw.

Most states have alcohol-free dry days or enforce degrees of Prohibition. Some upmarket restaurants may serve beer even if it's not listed, so it's worth asking. In some states there are government approved wine shops where you buy your alcohol through a metal grille. For dry states and liquor permits, see page 31.

Festivals and events

India has a wealth of festivals with many celebrated nationwide, while others are specific to a particular state or community or even a particular temple. Many fall on different dates each year depending on the Hindu lunar calendar so check with the tourist office.
➼ *Local festivals are listed in the Festivals and events section throughout the book.*

The Hindu calendar

Hindus follow two distinct eras: The *Vikrama Samvat* which began in 57 BC and the *Salivahan Saka* which dates from AD 78 and has been the official Indian calendar since 1957. The *Saka* new year starts on 22 March and has the same length as the Gregorian calendar. The 29½-day lunar month with its 'dark' and 'bright' halves based on the new and full moons, are named after 12 constellations, and total a 354-day year. The calendar cleverly has an extra month (*adhik maas*) every 2½ to three years, to bring it in line with the solar year of 365 days coinciding with the Gregorian calendar of the West.

Some major national and regional festivals are listed below. A few count as national holidays: **26 January**: Republic Day; **15 August**: Independence Day; **2 October**: Mahatma Gandhi's Birthday; **25 December**: Christmas Day.

Major festivals and fairs

Jan New Year's Day (**1 Jan**) is accepted officially when following the Gregorian calendar but there are regional variations which fall on different dates, often coinciding with spring/harvest time in Mar and Apr.
14 Jan Makar Sankranti marks the end of winter and is celebrated with kite flying.
Feb Vasant Panchami, the spring festival when people wear bright yellow clothes to mark the advent of the season with singing, dancing and feasting.
Feb-Mar Maha Sivaratri marks the night when Siva danced his celestial dance of destruction (*Tandava*), which is celebrated with feasting and fairs at Siva temples, but preceded by a night of devotional readings and hymn singing. **Carnival** in Goa. Spectacular costumes, music and dance, float processions and feasting mark the 3-day event.
Mar Holi, the festival of colours, marks the climax of spring. The previous night bonfires are lit symbolizing the end of winter (and conquering of evil). People have fun throwing coloured powder and water at each other and in the evening some gamble with friends. If you don't mind getting covered in colours,

you can risk going out but celebrations can sometimes get very rowdy (and unpleasant). Some worship Krishna who defeated the demon Putana.
Apr/May Buddha Jayanti, the 1st full moon night in Apr/May marks the birth of the Buddha.
Jul/Aug Raksha (or Rakhi) Bandhan symbolizes the bond between brother and sister, celebrated at full moon. A sister says special prayers for her brother and ties coloured threads around his wrist to remind him of the special bond. He in turn gives a gift and promises to protect and care for her. Sometimes *rakshas* are exchanged as a mark of friendship. **Narial Purnima** on the same full moon. Hindus make offerings of *narial* (coconuts) to the Vedic god Varuna (Lord of the waters) by throwing them into the sea.
15 Aug is **Independence Day**, a national secular holiday is marked by special events.
Ganesh Chaturthi was established just over 100 years ago by the Indian nationalist leader Tilak. The elephant-headed God of good omen is shown special reverence. On the last of the 5-day festival after harvest, clay images of Ganesh are taken in procession with dancers

and musicians, and are immersed in the sea, river or pond.

Aug/Sep Janmashtami, the birth of Krishna is celebrated at midnight at Krishna temples.

Sep/Oct Dasara has many local variations. Celebrations for the 9 nights *(navaratri)* are marked with **Ramlila**, various episodes of the Ramayana story are enacted with particular reference to the battle between the forces of good and evil. In some parts of India it celebrates *Rama's* victory over the Demon king *Ravana* of Lanka with the help of loyal *Hanuman* (Monkey). Huge effigies of *Ravana* made of bamboo and paper are burnt on the 10th day *(Vijaya dasami)* of **Dasara** in public open spaces. In some regions the focus is on Durga's victory over the demon *Mahishasura*.

Oct/Nov Gandhi Jayanti (**2 Oct**), Mahatma Gandhi's birthday, is remembered with prayer meetings and devotional singing.

Diwali/Deepavali *(Sanskrit ideepa* lamp), the festival of lights. Some Hindus celebrate Krishna's victory over the demon *Narakasura*, some Rama's return after his 14 years' exile in the forest when citizens lit his way with oil lamps. The festival falls on the dark *chaturdasi* (14th) night (the one preceding the new moon), when rows of lamps or candles are lit in remembrance, and *rangolis* are painted on the floor as a sign of welcome. Fireworks have become an integral part of the celebration which are often set off days before Diwali. Equally, Lakshmi, the Goddess of Wealth (as well as Ganesh) is worshipped by merchants and the business community who open the new financial year's account on the day. Most people wear new clothes; some play games of chance.

Guru Nanak Jayanti commemorates the birth of Guru Nanak. **Akhand Path** (unbroken reading of the holy book) takes place and the book itself (*Guru Granth Sahib*) is taken out in procession.

Dec Christmas Day (**25 Dec**) sees Indian Christians celebrate the birth of Christ in much the same way as in the West; many churches hold services/mass at midnight. There is an air of festivity in city markets which are specially decorated and illuminated. Over **New Year's Eve** (**31 Dec**) hotel prices peak and large supplements are added for meals and entertainment in the upper category hotels. Some churches mark the night with a Midnight Mass.

Muslim holy days

These are fixed according to the lunar calendar. According to the Gregorian calendar, they tend to fall 11 days earlier each year, dependent on the sighting of the new moon.

Ramadan is the start of the month of fasting when all Muslims (except young children, the very elderly, the sick, pregnant women and travellers) must abstain from food and drink, from sunrise to sunset.

Id ul Fitr is the 3-day festival that marks the end of Ramadan.

Id-ul-Zuha/Bakr-Id is when Muslims commemorate Ibrahim's sacrifice of his son according to God's commandment; the main time of pilgrimage to Mecca (the Hajj). It is marked by the sacrifice of a goat, feasting and alms giving.

Muharram is when the killing of the Prophet's grandson, Hussain, is commemorated by Shi'a Muslims. Decorated *tazias* (replicas of the martyr's tomb) are carried in procession by devout wailing followers who beat their chests to express their grief. Hyderabad and Lucknow are famous for their grand *tazias*. Shi'as fast for the 10 days.

Responsible travel

As well as respecting local cultural sensitivities, travellers can take a number of simple steps to reduce, or even improve, their impact on the local environment. Environmental concern is relatively new in India. Don't be afraid to pressurize businesses by asking about their policies.

Litter Many travellers think that there is little point in disposing of rubbish properly when the tossing of water bottles, plastic cups and other non-biodegradable items out of train windows is already so widespread. Don't follow an example you feel to be wrong. You can immediately reduce your impact by refusing plastic bags and other excess packaging when shopping – use a small backpack or cloth bag instead – and if you do collect a few, keep them with you to store other rubbish until you get to a litter bin.

Plastic mineral water bottles, an inevitable corollary to poor water hygiene standards, are a major contributor to India's litter mountain. However, many hotels, including nearly all of the upmarket ones, most restaurants and bus and train stations, provide drinking water purified using a combination of ceramic and carbon filters, chlorine and UV irradiation. Ask for '*filter paani*'; if the water tastes like a swimming pool it is probably quite safe to drink, though it's best to introduce your body gradually to the new water. If purifying water yourself, bringing it to a boil at sea level will make it safe, but at altitude you have to boil it for longer to ensure that all the microbes are killed. Various sterilizing methods can be used that contain chlorine (eg Puritabs) or iodine (eg Pota Aqua) and there are a number of mechanical or chemical water filters available on the market.

Bucket baths or showers The biggest issue relating to responsible and sustainable tourism is water. Much of northwest India is afflicted by severe water restrictions, with certain cities in Rajasthan and Gujarat having water supply for as little as 20 minutes a day. The traditional Indian 'bucket bath', in which you wet, soap then rinse off using a small hand-held plastic jug dipped into a large bucket, uses on average around 15 litres of water, as compared to 30-45 for a shower. These are commonly offered except in four- and five-star hotels.

Support responsible tourism Spending your money carefully can have a positive impact. Sleeping, eating and shopping at small, locally-owned businesses directly supports communities, while specific community tourism concerns, such as those operated by The **Blue Yonder** in Kerala and **Village Ways** in Uttarakhand, provide an economic motivation for people to stay in remote communities, protect natural areas and revive traditional cultures, rather than exploit the environment or move to the cities for work.

Transport Choose walking, cycling or public transport over fuel-guzzling cars and motorbikes.

Essentials A-Z

Accident and emergency

Contact the relevant emergency service (police T100, fire T101, ambulance T102) and your embassy (see under Directory in major cities). Make sure you obtain police/medical reports required for insurance claims.

Customs and duty free
Duty free

Tourists are allowed to bring in all personal effects 'which may reasonably be required', without charge. The official customs allowance includes 200 cigarettes or 50 cigars, 0.95 litres of alcohol, a camera and a pair of binoculars. Valuable personal effects and professional equipment including jewellery, special camera equipment and lenses, laptop computers and sound and video recorders must be declared on a Tourist Baggage Re-Export Form (TBRE) in order for them to be taken out of the country. These forms require the equipment's serial numbers. It saves considerable frustration if you know the numbers in advance and are ready to show them on the equipment. In addition to the forms, details of imported equipment may be entered into your passport. Save time by completing the formalities while waiting for your baggage. It is essential to keep these forms for showing to the customs when leaving India, otherwise considerable delays are very likely at the time of departure.

Prohibited items

The import of dangerous drugs, live plants, gold coins, gold and silver bullion and silver coins not in current use are either banned or subject to strict regulation. It is illegal to import firearms into India without special permission. Enquire at consular offices abroad for details.

Drugs

Certain areas, such as Goa's beaches, Kovalam, Gokarna and Hampi, have become associated with foreigners who take drugs. These are likely to attract local and foreign drug dealers but be aware that the government takes the misuse of drugs very seriously. Anyone charged with the illegal possession of drugs risks facing a fine of Rs 100,000 and a minimum 10 years' imprisonment. Several foreigners have been imprisoned for drugs-related offences in the last decade.

Electricity

Inida supply is 220-240 volts AC. Some top hotels have transformers. There may be pronounced variations in the voltage, and power cuts are common. Power back-up by generator or inverter is becoming more widespread, even in humble hotels, though it may not cover a/c. Socket sizes vary so take a universal adaptor; low-quality versions are available locally. Many hotels, even in the higher categories, don't have electric razor sockets. Invest in a stabilizer for a laptop.

Embassies and consulates

For information on visas and immigration, see page 30. For a comprehensive list of embassies (but not all consulates), see http://india.gov.in/overseas/indian_missions.php. Many embassies around the world are now outsourcing the visa process which might affect how long the process takes.

Health

Local populations in India are exposed to a range of health risks not encountered in the Western world. Many of the diseases are major problems for the local poor and destitute and, although the risk to travellers is more remote, they cannot be ignored. Obviously 5-star travel is going to carry less risk than backpacking on a budget.

Health care in the region is varied. There are many excellent private and government clinics/hospitals. As with all medical care, first impressions count. It's worth contacting your embassy or consulate on arrival and asking where the recommended (ie those used by diplomats) clinics are. You can also ask about locally recommended medical do's and don'ts. If you do get ill, and you have the opportunity, you should also ask your medical insurer whether they are satisfied that the medical centre/hospital you have been referred to is of a suitable standard.

Before you go

Ideally, you should see your GP or travel clinic at least 6 weeks before your departure for general advice on travel risks, malaria and vaccinations. Make sure you have travel insurance, get a dental check (especially if you are going to be away for more than a month), know your own blood group and if you suffer a long-term condition such as diabetes or epilepsy make sure someone knows or that you have a Medic Alert bracelet/necklace with this information on it. Remember that it is risky to buy medicinal tablets abroad because the doses may differ and India has a huge trade in false drugs.

Vaccinations

If you need vaccinations, see your doctor well in advance of your travel. Most courses must be completed by a minimum of 4 weeks. Travel clinics may provide rapid courses of vaccination, but are likely to be more expensive. The following vaccinations are recommended: typhoid, polio, tetanus, infectious hepatitis and diptheria. For details of malaria prevention, contact your GP or local travel clinic.

The following vaccinations may also be considered: rabies, possibly BCG (since TB is still common in the region) and in some cases meningitis and diphtheria (if you're staying in the country for a long time). Yellow fever is not required in India but you may be asked to show a certificate if you have travelled from Africa or South America. Japanese encephalitis may be required for rural travel at certain times of the year (mainly rainy seasons). An effective oral cholera vaccine (Dukoral) is now available as 2 doses providing 3 months' protection.

Websites

Blood Care Foundation (UK), www.bloodcare.org.uk A Kent-based charity 'dedicated to the provision of screened blood and resuscitation fluids in countries where these are not readily available'. They will dispatch certified non-infected blood of the right type to your hospital/clinic. The blood is flown in from various centres around the world.
British Travel Health Association (UK), www.btha.org This is the official website of an organization of travel health professionals.
Fit for Travel, www.fitfortravel.scot. nhs.uk This site from Scotland provides a quick A-Z of vaccine and travel health advice requirements for each country.
Foreign and Commonwealth Office (FCO) (UK), www.fco.gov.uk This is a key travel advice site, with useful information on the country, people, climate and lists the UK embassies/consulates. The site also promotes the concept of 'know before you go' and encourages travel insurance and appropriate travel health advice. It has links to Department of Health travel advice site.
The Health Protection Agency, www.hpa.org.uk Up-to-date malaria advice guidelines for travel around the world. It gives specific advice about the right drugs for each location. It also has useful information for those who are pregnant, suffering from epilepsy or planning to travel with children.

Medic Alert (UK), www.medicalalert.com
This is the website of the foundation that produces bracelets and necklaces for those with existing medical problems. Once you have ordered your bracelet/necklace you write your key medical details on paper inside it, so that if you collapse, a medic can identify you as having epilepsy or a nut allergy, etc.
Travel Screening Services (UK), www.travelscreening.co.uk   A private clinic dedicated to integrated travel health. The clinic gives vaccine, travel health advice, email and SMS text vaccine reminders and screens returned travellers for tropical diseases.
World Health Organisation, www.who. int   The WHO site has links to the *WHO Blue Book* on travel advice. This lists the diseases in different regions of the world. It describes vaccination schedules and makes clear which countries have yellow fever vaccination certificate requirements and malarial risk.

Books
International Travel and Health World Health Organisation Geneva, ISBN 92-4-15802-6-7.
Lankester, T, *The Travellers Good Health Guide*, ISBN 0-85969-827-0.
Warrell, D and Anderson, A (eds), *Expedition Medicine (The Royal Geographic Society)*, ISBN 1-86197-040-4.
Young Pelton, R, Aral, C and Dulles, W, *The World's Most Dangerous Places*, ISBN 1-566952-140-9.

Language
Hindi, spoken as a mother tongue by over 400 million people, is India's official language. The use of English is also enshrined in the Constitution for a wide range of official purposes, notably communication between Hindi and non-Hindi speaking states. The most widely spoken Indo-Aryan languages are: Bengali (8.3%), Marathi (8%), Urdu (5.7%), Gujarati (5.4%), Oriya (3.7%) and Punjabi (3.2%). Among the Dravidian languages Telugu (8.2%), Tamil (7%), Kannada (4.2%) and Malayalam (3.5%) are the most widely used. In Goa, Kokani and Marathi are the most common languages. See Language section, page 122, for useful words and phrases.

English now plays an important role across India. It is widely spoken in towns and cities and even in quite remote villages it is usually not difficult to find someone who speaks at least a little English. Outside of major tourist sites, other European languages are almost completely unknown. The accent in which English is spoken is often affected strongly by the mother tongue of the speaker and there have been changes in common grammar which sometimes make it sound unusual. Many of these changes have become standard Indian English usage, as valid as any other varieties of English used around the world. It is possible to study a number of Indian languages at language centres.

Money
Indian currency is the Indian Rupee (Re/Rs). It is **not** possible to purchase these before you arrive. If you want cash on arrival it is best to get it at the airport bank, although see if an ATM is available as airport rates are not very generous. Rupee notes are printed in denominations of Rs 1000, 500, 100, 50, 20, 10. The rupee is divided into 100 paise. Coins are minted in denominations of Rs 5, Rs 2, Rs 1 and 50 paise. **Note**   Carry money, mostly as traveller's cheques, in a money belt worn under clothing. Have a small amount in an easily accessible place.

Exchange rates *(Aug 2011)*
UK £1 = Rs 72.7, €1 = Rs 63.6, US$1 = Rs 44.3

Traveller's cheques (TCs)
TCs issued by reputable companies (eg **Thomas Cook**, **American Express**) are widely accepted. They can be easily exchanged at small local travel agents and tourist internet cafés but are rarely used

directly for payment. Try to avoid changing at banks, where the process can be time consuming; opt for hotels and agents instead, take large denomination cheques and change enough to last for some days. Most banks, but not all, will accept US dollars, pounds sterling and euro TCs so it is a good idea to carry some of each. Other major currency TCs are also accepted in some larger cities. One traveller warns that replacement of lost Amex TCs may take weeks. If travelling to remote areas it can be worth buying Indian rupee TCs from a major bank, these are more widely accepted than foreign currency ones.

Credit cards

Major credit cards are increasingly acceptable in the main centres, though in smaller cities and towns it is still rare to be able to pay by credit card. Payment by credit card can sometimes be more expensive than payment by cash, whilst some credit card companies charge a premium on cash withdrawals. **Visa** and **MasterCard** have a growing number of ATMs in major cities and several banks offer withdrawal facilities for Cirrus and Maestro cardholders. It is however easy to obtain a cash advance against a credit card. Railway reservation centres in major cities take payment for train tickets by Visa card which can be very quick as the queue is short, although they cannot be used for Tourist Quota tickets.

ATMs

By far the most convenient method of accessing money, ATMs are all over India, usually attended by security guards, with most banks offering some services to holders of overseas cards. Banks whose ATMs will issue cash against Cirrus and Maestro cards, as well as Visa and MasterCard, include **Bank of Baroda, Citibank, HDFC, HSBC, ICICI, IDBI, Punjab National Bank, State Bank of India (SBI), Standard Chartered** and **UTI**. A withdrawal fee is usually charged by the issuing bank on top of the conversion charges applied by your own bank. Fraud prevention measures quite often result in travellers having their cards blocked by the bank when unexpected overseas transactions occur; advise your bank of your travel plans before leaving.

Changing money

The **State Bank of India** and several others in major towns are authorized to deal in foreign exchange. Some give cash against Visa/MasterCard (eg **ANZ, Bank of Baroda** who print a list of their participating branches, **Andhra Bank**). American Express cardholders can use their cards to get either cash or TCs in Mumbai and Chennai. They also have offices in Coimbatore, Goa, Hyderabad, and Thiruvananthapuram. The larger cities have licensed money changers with offices usually in the commercial sector. Changing money through unauthorized dealers is illegal. Premiums on the currency black market are very small and highly risky. Large hotels change money 24 hrs a day for guests, but banks often give a substantially better rate of exchange. It is best to exchange money on arrival at the airport bank or the Thomas Cook counter. Many international flights arrive during the night and it is generally far easier and less time consuming to change money at the airport than in the city. You should be given a foreign currency encashment certificate when you change money through a bank or authorized dealer; ask for one if it is not automatically given. It allows you to change Indian rupees back to your own currency on departure. It also enables you to use rupees to pay hotel bills or buy air tickets for which payment in foreign exchange may be required. The certificates are only valid for 3 months.

Cost of living

The cost of living in India remains well below that in the West. The average wage per capita is about Rs 34,000 per year (US$800). Manual, unskilled labourers (women are often paid less than men), farmers and others in rural areas earn considerably less. However, thanks to booming global demand for workers who can provide cheaper IT and technology support functions and many Western firms transferring office functions or call centres to India, salaries in certain sectors have sky rocketed. An IT specialist can earn an average Rs 500,000 per year and upwards – a rate that is rising by around 15% a year.

Cost of travelling

Most food, accommodation and public transport, especially rail and bus, is exceptionally cheap, although inflation in 2010 was 16.3% and basic food items such as rice, lentils, tomatoes and onions have skyrocketed. There is a widening range of moderately priced but clean hotels and restaurants outside the big cities, making it possible to get a great deal for your money. Budget travellers sharing a room, taking public transport, avoiding souvenir stalls, and eating nothing but rice and dhal can get away with a budget of Rs 400-600 (about US$8-12 or £5-8) a day. This sum leaps up if you drink alcohol (still cheap by European standards at about US$2, £1 or Rs 80 for a pint), smoke foreign-brand cigarettes or want to have your own wheels (you can expect to spend between Rs 150 and 200 to hire a Honda per day). Those planning to stay in fairly comfortable hotels and use taxis sightseeing should budget at US$50-80 (£30-50) a day. Then again you could always check into **Ananda Spa** or the **Taj Falaknuma** for Christmas and notch up an impressive US$600 (£350) bill on your B&B alone. India can be a great place to pick and choose, save a little on basic accommodation and then treat yourself to the type of meal you could only dream of affording back home. Also, be prepared to spend a fair amount more in Mumbai, Hyderabad, Bengaluru (Bangalore) and Chennai, where not only is the cost of living significantly higher but where it's worth coughing up extra for a half-decent room:

penny-pinch by the beach when you'll be spending precious little time indoors anyway. A newspaper costs Rs 5 and breakfast for 2 with coffee can come to as little as Rs 50 in a South Indian 'hotel', but if you intend to eat banana pancakes or pasta beside a Goan beach, you can expect to pay more like Rs 50-150 a plate.

Opening hours

Banks are open Mon-Fri 1030-1430, Sat 1030-1230. Top hotels sometimes have a 24-hr money changing service. **Post offices** open Mon-Fri 1000-1700, often shutting for lunch, and Sat mornings. **Government offices** Mon-Fri 0930-1700, Sat 0930-1300 (some open on alternate Sat only). **Shops** open Mon-Sat 0930-1800. Bazars keep longer hours.

Post

The post is frequently unreliable, and delays are common. It is best to use a post office where you can hand over mail for franking across the counter, or a top hotel post box. Valuable items should only be sent by registered mail. Government emporia or shops in the larger hotels will send purchases home if the items are difficult to carry. Seamail and Book Post have been on hold since Jan 2008 because of the Somali pirate situation – best to check for availability.

Airmail services to Europe, Africa and Australia take at least a week and a little longer for the Americas. **Speed post** (which takes about 4 days to the UK) is available from major towns. Speed post to the UK from Tamil Nadu costs Rs 675 for the first 250 g sent and an extra Rs 75 for each 250 g thereafter. **Courier services** (eg DHL) are available in the larger towns. At some main post offices you can send small packages under 2 kg as **letter post** (rather than parcel post), which is much cheaper at Rs 220. Check that the post office holds necessary customs declaration forms

(2-3 copies needed). Write 'No commercial value' if returning used clothes, books, etc. **Sea mail** costs Rs 800 for 10 kg. 'Packers' at or near the post office do necessary cloth covering, sealing etc for Rs 20-50; you address the parcel, obtain stamps from a separate counter; stick stamps and a customs form to the parcel with the provided glue (the other form/s must be partially sewn on). Post at the Parcels Counter and obtain a registration slip. Cost varies by destination and is normally displayed on a board beside the counter. Specialist shippers deal with larger items, normally around US$150 per cubic metre. Sea mail is currently being phased out to be replaced by **SAL** (Surface Air Lifted). The prices are fractionally lower than airmail, Rs 500-600 for the first kg and Rs 150-250 per extra kg. Delivery can take up to 2 months.

Poste restante facilities are widely available in even quite small towns at the GPO where mail is held for 1 month. Ask for mail to be addressed to you with your surname in capitals and underlined. When asking for mail at Poste Restante check under surname as well as christian name.

Safety
Personal security

In general the threats to personal security for travellers in India are remarkably small. However, incidents of petty theft and violence directed specifically at tourists have been on the increase so care is necessary in some places, and basic common sense needs to be used with respect to looking after valuables. Follow the same precautions you would when at home. There have been incidents of sexual assault in and around the main tourist beach centres, particularly after full moon parties in South India. Avoid wandering alone outdoors late at night in these places. During daylight hours be careful in remote places, especially when alone. If you are under threat, scream loudly. Be very

cautious before accepting food or drink from casual acquaintances, as it may be drugged.

The left-wing Maoist extremist Naxalites are active in east central and southern India. They have a long history of conflict with state and national authorities, including attacks on police and government officials. The Naxalites have not specifically targeted Westerners, but have attacked symbolic targets including Western companies. As a general rule, travellers are advised to be vigilant in the lead up to and on days of national significance, such as Republic Day (26 Jan) and Independence Day (15 Aug) as militants have in the past used such occasions to mount attacks.

Following a major explosion on the Delhi to Lahore (Pakistan) train in Feb 2007 and the Mumbai attacks in Nov 2008, increased security has been implemented on many trains and stations. Similar measures at airports may cause delays for passengers so factor this into your timing. Also check your airline's website for up-to-date information on luggage restrictions. In Mumbai, the UK's Foreign and Commonwealth Office warns of a risk of armed robbers holding up taxis travelling along the main highway from the airport to the city in the early hours of the morning (0200-0600) when there is little traffic on the roads. If you are using the route during these times, you should, if possible, arrange to travel by coach or seek advice at the airport on arrival.

That said, in the great majority of places visited by tourists, violent crime and personal attacks are extremely rare.

Travel advice

It is better to seek advice from your consulate than from travel agencies. Before you travel you can contact: **British Foreign & Commonwealth Office Travel Advice Unit**, T0845-850 2829 (Pakistan desk T020-7270 2385), www.fco.gov.uk. **US State Department's Bureau of Consular Affairs**, Overseas Citizens

Services, Room 4800, Department of State, Washington, DC 20520-4818, USA, T202-647 1488, http://travel.state.gov. **Australian Department of Foreign Affairs Canberra**, Australia, T02-6261 3305, www.smartraveller.gov.au. Canadian official advice is on www.voyage.gc.ca.

Theft

Theft is not uncommon. It is best to keep TCs, passports and valuables with you at all times. Don't regard hotel rooms as being automatically safe; even hotel safes don't guarantee secure storage. Avoid leaving valuables near open windows even when you are in the room. Use your own padlock in a budget hotel when you go out. Pickpockets and other thieves operate in the big cities. Crowded areas are particularly high risk. Take special care of your belongings when getting on or off public transport.

If you have items stolen, they should be reported to the police as soon as possible. Keep a separate record of vital documents, including passport details and numbers of TCs. Larger hotels will be able to assist in contacting and dealing with the police. Dealings with the police can be very difficult and in the worst regions, such as Bihar, even dangerous. The paperwork involved in reporting losses can be time consuming and irritating and your own documentation (eg passport and visas) may be demanded.

In some states the police occasionally demand bribes, though you should not assume that if procedures move slowly you are automatically being expected to offer a bribe. The traffic police are tightening up on traffic offences in some places. They have the right to make on-the-spot fines for speeding and illegal parking. If you face a fine, insist on a receipt. If you have to go to a police station, try to take someone with you.

If you face really serious problems (eg in connection with a driving accident), contact your consular office as quickly as possible.

You should ensure you always have your international driving licence and motorbike or car documentation with you.

Confidence tricksters are particularly common where people are on the move, notably around railway stations or places where budget tourists gather. A common plea is some sudden and desperate calamity; sometimes a letter will be produced in English to back up the claim. The demands are likely to increase sharply if sympathy is shown.

Telephone

The international code for India is +91. International Direct Dialling is widely available in privately run call booths, usually labelled on yellow boards with the letters 'PCO-STD-ISD'. You dial the call yourself, and the time and cost are displayed on a computer screen. Cheap rate (2100-0600) means long queues may form outside booths. Telephone calls from hotels are usually more expensive (check price before calling), though some will allow local calls free of charge. Internet phone booths, usually associated with cybercafés, are the cheapest way of calling overseas.

A double ring repeated regularly means it is ringing; equal tones with equal pauses means engaged (similar to the UK). If calling a mobile, rather than ringing, you might hear music while you wait for an answer.

One disadvantage of the tremendous pace of the telecommunications revolution is the fact that millions of telephone numbers go out of date every year. Current telephone directories themselves are often out of date and some of the numbers given in this book will have been changed even as we go to press. Our best advice is if the number in the text does not work, add a '2'. **Directory enquiries**, T197, can be helpful but works only for the local area code.

Mobile phones are for sale everywhere, as are local SIM cards that allow you to make calls within India and overseas at much lower rates than using a 'roaming' service from your normal provider at home – sometimes for as little as Rs 0.5 per min. Arguably the best service is provided by the government carrier **BSNL/MTNL** but security provisions make connecting to the service virtually impossible for foreigners. Private companies such as **Airtel**, **Vodafone**, **Reliance** and **Tata Indicom** are easier to sign up with, but the deals they offer can be befuddling and are frequently changed. To connect you'll need to complete a form, have a local address or receipt showing the address of your hotel, and present photocopies of your passport and visa plus 2 passport photos to an authorized reseller – most phone dealers will be able to help, and can also sell top-up. **Univercell**, www.univercell.in, and **The Mobile Store**, www.themobilestore.in, are 2 widespread and efficient chains selling phones and sim cards.

India is divided into a number of 'calling circles' or regions, and if you travel outside the region where your connection is based, eg from Delhi into Rajasthan, you will pay higher charges for making and receiving calls, and any problems that may occur – with 'unverified' documents, for example – can be much harder to resolve.

Time

India doesn't change its clocks, so from the last Sun in Oct to the last Sun in Mar the time is GMT +5½ hrs, and the rest of the year it's +4½ hrs (USA, EST +10½ and +9½ hrs; Australia, EST -5½ and -4½ hrs).

Tipping

A tip of Rs 10 to a bellboy carrying luggage in a modest hotel (Rs 20 in a higher category) would be appropriate. In upmarket restaurants, a 10% tip is acceptable when service is not already included, while in places serving very cheap meals, round off the bill with small change. Indians don't normally tip taxi drivers but a small extra is welcomed. Porters at

airports and railway stations often have a fixed rate displayed but will usually press for more. Ask fellow passengers what a fair rate is.

Tourist information

There are **Government of India** tourist offices in the state capitals, as well as state tourist offices (sometimes **Tourism Development Corporations**) in the major cities and a few important sites. They produce their own tourist literature, either free or sold at a nominal price, and some also have lists of city hotels and paying guest options. The quality of material is improving though maps are often poor. Many offer tours of the city, neighbouring sights and overnight and regional packages. Some run modest hotels and midway motels with restaurants and may also arrange car hire and guides. The staff in the regional and local offices are usually helpful.

Tourist offices overseas

Australia Level 5, Glasshouse,135 King St, Sydney, NSW 2000, T02-9221 9555, info@indiatourism.com.au.
Canada 60 Bloor St West, Suite No 1003, Toronto, Ontario, T416-962 3787, indiatourism@bellnet.ca.
Dubai 6 Post Box 12856, NASA Building, Al Maktoum Rd, Deira, T04-227 4848, goirto@emirates.net.ae.
France 11-13 Bis Boulevard Hausmann, 75009, Paris T01-4523 3045.
Germany Baserler St 48, 60329, Frankfurt AM-Main 1, T069-242 9490, www.india-tourism.de.
Italy Via Albricci 9, Milan 20122, T02-805 3506, info@indiatourismmilan.com.
Japan B9F Chiyoda Building, 1-8-17 Ginza, Chuo-Ku, Tokyo 104-0061, T03-3561 0651, indiatourt@smile.ocn.ne.jp.
The Netherlands Rokin 9-15, 1012 KK Amsterdam, T020-620 8991, info@indiatourismamsterdam.com.

Singapore 20 Kramat Lane, 01-01A United House, 228773, Singapore, T6235-3800, indtour.sing@pacific.net.sg.
South Africa Hyde Lane, Lancaster Gate, Johannesburg, T011-325 0880, goito@global.co.za.
UK 7 Cork St, London WIS 3LH, T020-74373677, T08700-102183, london5@indiatouristoffice.org.
USA 3550 Wilshire Blvd, Room 204, Los Angeles, California 90010, T213-380 8855, goitola@aol.com; Suite 1808, 1270 Av of Americas, New York, NY 10020-1700, T212-5864901, ny@itonyc.com. Also check out www.incredibleindia.org for information.

Visas and immigration

For embassies and consulates, see page 22. Virtually all foreign nationals, including children, require a visa to enter India. Nationals of Bhutan and Nepal only require a suitable means of identification. The rules regarding visas change frequently and arrangements for application and collection also vary from town to town so it is essential to check details and costs with the relevant embassy or consulate. These remain closed on Indian national holidays. Now many consulates and embassies are outsourcing the visa process, it's best to find out in advance how long it will take. For example, in London where you used to be able to get a visa in person in a morning if you were prepared to queue, it now takes 2-3 working days and involves 2 trips to the office.

At other offices, it can be much easier to apply in advance by post, to avoid queues and frustratingly low visa quotas. Postal applications can 15 working days to process.

Visitors from countries with no Indian representation may apply to the resident British representative, or enquire at the **Air India** office. An application on the prescribed form should be accompanied by 2 passport photographs and your passport which should be valid 6 months beyond the period of your visit. Note that visas are valid from the date granted, not from the date of entry. For up-to-date information on visa requirements visit www.india-visa.com.

No foreigner needs to register within the 180-day period of their tourist visa. All foreign visitors who stay in India for more than 180 days need to get an income tax clearance exemption certificate from the Foreign Section of the Income Tax Department in Delhi, Mumbai, Kolkata or Chennai.

Currently the following visa rules apply:
Transit For passengers en route to another country (no more than 72 hrs in India).
Tourist Normally valid for 3-6 months from date of issue, though some nationalities may be granted visas for up to 5 years. Multiple entries permitted, but a new rule requires a 2-month wait before you can return to India. The rule doesn't apply if you plan to visit neighbouring countries as part of your trip (eg Nepal, Sri Lanka), but you need clear documentation proving your itinerary.
Business 3-6 months or up to 2 years with multiple entry. A letter from the company giving the nature of business is required.
5 year For those of Indian origin only, who have held Indian passports.
Student Valid up to 1 year from the date of issue. Attach a letter of acceptance from Indian institution and an AIDS test certificate. Allow up to 3 months for approval.
Visa extensions Applications should be made to the Foreigners' Regional Registration Offices at New Delhi, Mumbai, Kolkata or Chennai, or an office of the Superintendent of Police in the District Headquarters. After 6 months, you must leave India and apply for a new visa – the Nepal office is known to be difficult. Anyone staying in India for a period of more than 180 days (6 months) must register at a convenient Foreigners' Registration Office.

Work permits

Foreigners should apply to the Indian representative in their country of origin for the latest information about work permits.

Liquor permits

Periodically some Indian states have tried to enforce prohibition. To some degree it is in force in Gujarat, Manipur, Mizoram and Nagaland. When applying for your visa you can ask for an All India Liquor Permit. Foreigners can also get the permit from any Government of India Tourist Office in Delhi or the state capitals. Instant permits are issued by some hotels.

Weights and measures

Metric is in universal use in the cities. In remote areas local measures are sometimes used. One lakh is 100,000 and 1 crore is 10 million.

Women travellers

Independent travel is still largely unheard of for Indian women. Although it is relatively safe for women to travel around India, most people find it an advantage to travel with a companion. Even then, privacy is rarely respected and there can be a lot of hassle, pressure and intrusion on your personal space, as well as some outright harassment. Backpackers setting out alone often meet like-minded travelling companions at budget hotels. Cautious women travellers recommend dying blonde hair black and wearing wedding rings, but the most important measure to ensure respect is to dress appropriately, in loose-fitting, non-see-through clothes, covering shoulders, arms and legs (such as a *salwaar kameez*,

which can be made to fit in around 24 hrs for around Rs 400-800). Take advantage, too, of the gender segregation on public transport, to avoid hassle and to talk to local women. In mosques women should be covered from head to ankle. **Independent Traveller**, T0870-760 5001, www.independent traveller.com, runs women-only tours to India.

'Eve teasing', the euphemism for physical harassment, is an unfortunate result of the sexual repression latent in Indian culture, combined with a young male population whose only access to sex education is via the dingy cybercafés. Unaccompanied women are most vulnerable in major cities, crowded bazars, beach resorts and tourist centres where men may follow them and touch them; festival nights are particularly bad for this. Women have reported that they have been molested while being measured for clothing in tailors' shops. If you are harassed, it can be effective to make a scene. Be firm and clear if you don't wish to speak to someone. The best response to staring, whether lascivious or curious, is to avert your eyes down and away. This is not the submissive gesture it might seem, but an effective tool to communicate that you have no interest in any further interaction. Aggressively staring back or confronting the starer can be construed as a come-on. It is best to be accompanied at night, especially when travelling by rickshaw or taxi in towns. Be prepared to raise an alarm if anything unpleasant threatens.

Most railway booking offices have separate women's ticket queues or ask women to go to the head of the general queue. Some buses have seats reserved for women.

Contents

Goa

Footprint features

At a glance

🚍 **Getting around** Goa is rickshaw free. Local buses, chartered mini-buses, taxis and motorbike taxis are all the norm. Hiring your own Honda or Enfield is a popular option.

⏱ **Time required** Allow 1 day for Old Goa, 1 day for the palaces of the south: and 3 days' round-trip for Hampi (in Karnataka). Then factor in beach time: some tire of Goa's beaches after 1-2 days, some spend a fortnight, some never leave.

☁ **Weather** Chilly evenings in Dec and Jan, best Oct-Feb. Humidity rises from Mar.

✖ **When not to go** Avoid monsoon and peak season (Christmas and New Year) when prices sky rocket as the state opens up for the domestic Indian tourist's equivalent of 'Spring Break'.

Panjim (Panaji) and Old Goa

Sleepy, dusty Panjim was adopted as the Portuguese capital when the European empire was already on the wane, and the colonizers left little in the way of lofty architecture. A tiny city with a Riviera-style promenade along the Mandovi, it's also splendidly uncommercial: the biggest business seems to be in the sale of kaju (cashews), gentlemen-shaves in the barbieris and feni-quaffing in the booths of pokey bars – and city folk still insist on sloping off for a siesta at lunch. The 18th- and 19th-century bungalows clustered in the neighbouring quarters of San Thome and Fontainhas stand as the victims of elegant architectural neglect. Further upriver, a thick swathe of jungle – wide fanning raintrees, the twists of banyan branches and coconut palms – has drawn a heavy, dusty blanket over the relics of the doomed Portuguese capital of Old Goa, a ghost town of splendid rococo and baroque ecclesiastical edifices.

Ins and outs

Getting there Pre-paid taxis or buses run the short distance from Dabolim airport across Mormugao Bay to Panjim. The closest station on the Konkan Railway is at Karmali, 10 km east, with trains from Mumbai to the north and coastal Karnataka and Kerala to the south; taxis and buses run from Karmali to Panjim. The state-run Kadamba buses and private coach terminals are in Patto to the east of town. From there it is a 10-minute walk across the footbridge over the Ourem Creek to reach the city's guesthouses. ▸▸ *See Transport, page 48.*

Getting around Panjim holds the archbishop's palace, a modern port and government buildings and shops set around a number of plazas. It is laid out on a grid and the main roads run parallel with the seafront. The area is very easy to negotiate on foot, but autos are readily available. Motorcycle rickshaws are cheaper but slightly more risky. Local buses run along the waterfront from the City Bus Stand past the market and on to Miramar.

Tourist information Goa Tourism Development Corporation (GTDC) ① *east bank of the Ourem Creek, beside the bus stand at Patto, T0832-243 8750, www.goa-tourism.com, Mon-Sat 0900-1130, 1330-1700, Sun 0930-1400.* Also has an information counter at Dabolim airport, and runs a moderately helpful information line, T0832-241 2121. India Tourism ① *Church Sq, T0832-222 3412, www.incredibleindia.com.*

Panaji is the official spelling of the capital city, replacing the older Portuguese spelling Panjim. It is still most commonly referred to as Panjim, so we have followed usage.

History

The Portuguese first settled Panjim as a suburb of Old Goa, the original Indian capital of the sea-faring *conquistadores*, but its position on the left bank of the Mandovi River had already attracted Bijapur's Muslim king Yusuf Adil Shah in 1500, shortly before the Europeans arrived. He built and fortified what the Portuguese later renamed the Idalcao Palace, now the oldest and most impressive of downtown Panjim's official buildings. The palace's service to the sultan was short-lived: Alfonso de Albuquerque seized it, and Old Goa upstream – which the Islamic rulers had been using as both a trading port and their main starting point for pilgrimages to Mecca – in March 1510. Albuquerque, like his Muslim predecessors, built his headquarters in Old Goa, and proceeded to station a garrison at Panjim and made it the customs clearing point for all traffic entering the Mandovi.

The town remained little more than a military outpost and a staging post for incoming and outgoing viceroys on their way to Old Goa. The first Portuguese buildings, after the construction of a church on the site of the present Church of Our Lady of Immaculate Conception in 1541, were noblemen's houses built on the flat land bordering the sea. Panjim had to wait over two centuries – when the Portuguese Viceroy decided to move from Old Goa in 1759 – for settlement to begin in earnest. It then took the best part of a century for enough numbers to relocate from Old Goa to make Panjim the biggest settlement in the colony and to warrant its status as official capital in 1833.

Sights

The waterfront → *For listings, see pages 44-49.*

The leafy boulevard of Devanand Bandodkar (DB) Marg runs along the Mandovi from near the New Patto Bridge in the east to the Campal to the southwest. When Panjim's transport and communication system depended on boats, this was its busiest highway and it still holds the city's main administrative buildings and its colourful market.

Walking from the east, you first hit **Idalcao Palace** ① *behind the main boat terminal, DB Marg*. Once the castle of the Adil Shahs, the palace was seized by the Portuguese when they first toppled the Muslim kings in 1510 and was rebuilt in 1615 to serve as the

Panjim

Europeans' Viceregal Palace. It was the official residence to Viceroys from 1759 right up until 1918 when the governor-general (the viceroy's 20th-century title) decided to move to the Cabo headland to the southwest – today's Cabo Raj Niwas – leaving the old palace to become government offices. After Independence it became Goa's secretariat building (the seat of the then Union Territory's parliament) until that in turn shifted across the river to Porvorim. It now houses the bureaucracy of the state passport office. Next to it is a striking dark statue of the **Abbé Faria** (1756-1819) looming over the prone figure of a woman. José Custodio de Faria, who went on to become a celebrated worldwide authority on hypnotism, was born into a Colvale Brahmin family in Candolim. The character in Dumas' Count of Monte Cristo may have been based on this Abbé.

Further west, on Malacca Road, almost opposite the wharf, are the central library and public rooms of the **Braganza Institute** ⓘ *Mon-Fri 0930-1300, 1400-1745*. It was

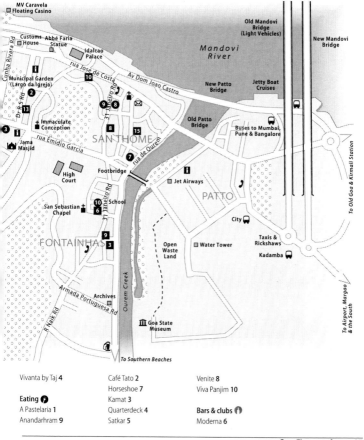

Vivanta by Taj 4	Café Tato 2	Venite 8
	Horseshoe 7	Viva Panjim 10
Eating 🍴	Kamat 3	
A Pastelaria 1	Quarterdeck 4	**Bars & clubs** 🍸
Anandarhram 9	Satkar 5	Moderna 6

established as the Instituto Vasco da Gama in 1871 (the anniversary of the date that the Portuguese explorer da Gama sailed round the Cape of Good Hope), to stimulate an interest in culture, science and the arts. It was renamed for Luis Menezes de Braganza (1878-1938), an outstanding figure of social and political reform in early 20th-century Goa. The blue tile frieze in the entrance, hand painted by Jorge Colaco in 1935, is a mythical representation of the Portuguese colonization of Goa. An art gallery upstairs has paintings by European artists of the late 19th and early 20th centuries and Goan artists of the 20th century. The **central library** ① *0930-1300, 1200-1700*, dating from 1832, has a rare collection of religious and other texts.

City centre → *For listings, see pages 44-49.*

The giant whitewashed 16th-century **Church of the Immaculate Conception** ① *Church Sq, Emidio Gracia Rd, Mon-Sat 0900-1230, 1530-1730, Sun 1100-1230, 1530-1700, free, English Mass Mon-Fri 0800, Sun 0830*, looms pristine and large up a broad sweep of steps off the main square, Largo Da Igreja, blue and white flags fluttering at its fringes. Its dimensions were unwarranted for the population of what was at the time of its construction in 1541, in Panjim, little more than a marshy fishing village; its tall, Portuguese baroque twin towers were instead built both to act as a landmark for and to tend to the spiritual needs of arriving Portuguese sailors, for whom the customs post just below the hill at Panjim marked their first step on Indian soil. The church was enlarged in 1600 to reflect its status as parish church of the capital and in 1619 was rebuilt to its present design. Inside is an ornate jewel in Goan Catholicism's trademark blue, white and gold, wood carved into gilt corkscrews, heavy chandeliers and chintz. The classic baroque main altar *reredos* (screens) are sandwiched between altars to Jesus the Crucified and to Our Lady of the Rosary, in turn flanked by marble statues of St Peter and St Paul. The panels in the Chapel of St Francis, in the south transept, came from the chapel in the Idalcao Palace in 1918. Parishioners bought the statue of Our Lady of Fatima her crown of gold and diamonds in 1950 (candlelight procession every 13 October). The church's feast day is on 8 December.

The Hindu **Mahalaxmi Temple** ① *Dr Dada Vaidya Rd, free,* (originally 1818, but rebuilt and enlarged in 1983) is now hidden behind a newer building. It was the first Hindu place of worship to be allowed in the Old Conquests after the close of the Inquisition. The **Boca de Vaca** ('Cow's Mouth') spring, is nearby.

San Thome and Fontainhas → *For listings, see pages 44-49.*

On Panjim's eastern promontory, at the foot of the Altinho and on the left bank of the Ourem Creek, sit first the San Thome and then, further south, Fontainhas districts filled with modest 18th- and 19th-century houses. The cumulative prettiness of the well-preserved buildings' colour-washed walls, trimmed with white borders, sloping tiled roofs and decorative wrought-iron balconies make it an ideal area to explore on foot. You can reach the area via any of the narrow lanes that riddle San Thome or take the footbridge across the Ourem Creek from the New Bus Stand and tourist office that feeds you straight into the heart of the district. A narrow road that runs east past the Church of the Immaculate Conception and main town square also ends up here. But probably the best way in is over the Altinho from the Mahalaxmi Temple: this route gives great views over the estuary from the steep eastern flank of the hill, a vantage point that was once used for defensive purposes. A footpath drops down between the Altinho's 19th- and 20th-century buildings just south of San Sebastian Chapel to leave you slap bang in middle of Fontainhas.

The chief landmark here is the small **San Sebastian Chapel** ⓘ *St Sebastian Rd, open only during Mass held in Konkani Mon-Tue, Thu-Sat 0715-0800, Wed 1800-1900, Sun 0645-0730, English Mass Sun 0830-0930, free,* (built 1818, rebuilt 1888) which houses the large wooden crucifix that until 1812 stood in the Palace of the Inquisition in Old Goa where the eyes of Christ watched over the proceedings of the tribunal. Before being moved here, it was in Idalcao Palace's chapel in Panjim for 100 years.

The **Goa State Museum** ⓘ *Patto, 0930-1730, free, head south of Kadamba Bus Stand, across the Ourem Creek footbridge, right across the waste ground and past the State Bank staff training building,* is an impressive building that contains a disappointingly small collection of religious art and antiquities. Most interesting are the original Provedoria lottery machines built in Lisbon that are on the first floor landing. A few old photos show how the machines were used.

Old Goa and around → *For listings, see pages 44-49.*

The white spires of Old Goa's glorious ecclesiastical buildings burst into the Indian sky from the depths of overgrown jungle that has sprawled where admirals and administrators of the Portuguese Empire once tended the oriental interests of their 16th-century King Manuel. The canopies of a hundred raintrees cast their shade across the desolate streets, adding to the romantic melancholy beauty of the deserted capital.

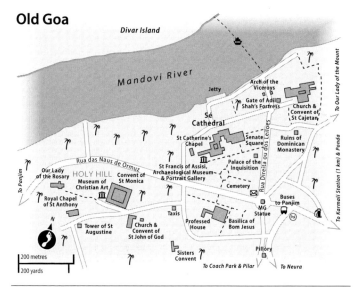

Old Goa

Divar Island

Mandovi River

Jetty

Arch of the Viceroys

Gate of Adil Shah's Fortress

Church & Convent of St Cajetan

To Our Lady of the Mount

Sé Cathedral

St Catherine's Chapel

Senate Square

Ruins of Dominican Monastery

Rua das Naus de Ormuz

St Francis of Assisi, Archaeological Museum & Portrait Gallery

Palace of the Inquisition

To Karmali Station (1 km) & Ponda

Our Lady of the Rosary

HOLY HILL

Museum of Christian Art

Convent of St Monica

Cemetery

Buses to Panjim

To Panjim

Royal Chapel of St Anthony

Rua Direita ou dos Leilões

MG Statue

Tower of St Augustine

Church & Convent of St John of God

Taxis

Professed House

Basilica of Bom Jesus

Pillory

200 metres

200 yards

Sisters Convent

To Coach Park & Pilar

To Neura

Tourists and pilgrims continue to flock to the remains of St Francis Xavier in the giddying baroque Basilica of Bom Jesus, where hawkers thrust spindly votive candles into their hands and compete to slake thirsts with fresh coconut, lime or sugarcane juice.

Ins and outs

Getting there Old Goa lies on the south bank of the Mandovi on the crest of a low hill 8 km from Panjim. The frequent bus service takes 15-20 minutes. Buses drop you off opposite the Basilica of Bom Jesus (Rs 5); pick up the return bus near the police station. Auto-rickshaws charge Rs 25, taxis Rs 150 return. Karmali station on the Konkan Railway, just east of the centre, has taxis for transfers.

Getting around The major monuments are within easy walking distance of the bus stop. All monuments are open daily year-round 0830-1730.

History

Old Goa is to Christians the spiritual heart of the territory. It owes its origin as a Portuguese capital to Afonso de Albuquerque and some of its early ecclesiastical development to St Francis Xavier who was here, albeit for only five months, in the mid-16th century. Before the Portuguese arrived it was the second capital of the Muslim Bijapur Kingdom. Today, all the mosques and fortifications of that period have disappeared and only a fragment of the Sultan's palace walls remain.

Under the Portuguese, Old Goa was grand enough to be dubbed the 'Rome of the East', but it was a flourishing port with an enviable trade even before the Portuguese arrived. The bustling walled city was peopled by merchants of many nationalities who came to buy and sell horses from Arabia and Hormuz, to trade silk, muslin, calico, rice, spices and areca nuts from the interior and other ports along the west coast. It was a centre of shipbuilding and boasted fine residences and public buildings.

After the arrival of the Portuguese, Old Goa swelled still further in size and significance. In the west lay barracks, mint, foundry and arsenal, hospital and prison. The banks of the Mandovi held the shipyards of Ribeira des Gales and next door lay the administrative and commercial centre. Streets and areas of the city were set aside for different activities and merchandise, each with its own character. The most important, Rua Direita ou dos Leiloes (Straight Street), was lined with jewellers, bankers and artisans. It was also the venue for auctions of precious goods, held every morning except Sunday. To the east was the market and the old fortress of Adil Shah, while the true centre of the town was filled with magnificent churches built by the Franciscans, themselves joined by waves of successive religious orders: first the Dominicans in 1548, the Augustinians from 1572, the Carmelites from 1612 and finally the Theatines from 1655. By the mid-17th century, the city, plagued by cholera and malaria and crippled economically, was abandoned for Panjim.

Basilica of Bom Jesus

The Renaissance façade of Goa's most famous church, the Basilica of Bom (the Good) Jesus, a UNESCO World Heritage Site, reflects the architectural transition to baroque then taking place in Europe. Apart from the elaborate gilded altars, wooden pulpit and the candy-twist Bernini columns, the interior is very simple.

The church has held the treasured remains of **St Francis Xavier**, a former pupil of soldier-turned-saint Ignatius Loyola, the founder of the Order of Jesuits since the 17th century. Francis's canonization was in 1622.

The tomb, which lies to the right of the main chancel (1698), was the gift of one of the last of the Medicis, Cosimo III, Grand Duke of Tuscany, and took the Florentine sculptor Giovanni Batista Foggini 10 years to complete. It is made of three tiers of marble and jasper; the upper tier holds scenes from the saint's life. The casket is silver and has three locks, the keys being held by the Governor, the Archbishop and the Convent Administrator. You can look down on to the tomb from a small window in the art gallery next to the church.

After his canonization, St Francis's body was shown on each anniversary of his death until 1707, when it was restricted to a few special private expositions. In 1752, the cadaver was again paraded to quash rumours that the Jesuits had removed it. The exhibition now happens every 10 to 12 years (the last exposition was in 2005), when the relics are taken to the Sé Cathedral. Feast Day is 3 December.

Sé Cathedral

Across the square sits the Sé Cathedral, dedicated to St Catherine on whose day (25 November) Goa was recaptured by Albuquerque. Certainly the largest church in Old Goa, it could even be the biggest in Asia and was built on the ruins of a mosque by the Dominicans between 1562 and 1623. The building is Tuscan outside and Corinthian inside, with a barrel-vaulted ceiling and east-facing main façade. One of the characteristic twin towers collapsed in 1776 when it was struck by lightning. The remaining tower holds five bells including the Golden Bell (cast in Cuncolim in 1652). The vast interior, divided into the barrel-vaulted nave with clerestory and two side aisles, has a granite baptismal font. On each side of the church are four chapels along the aisles; on the right, these are dedicated to St Anthony, St Bernard, the Cross of Miracles and the Holy Spirit, and on the left, starting at the entrance, to Our Lady of Virtues, St Sebastian, the Blessed Sacrament and Our Lady of Life. The clerestory windows are protected by a shield crowned by a balustrade to keep out the sun. The main altar is superbly gilded and painted, with six further altars in the transept. The marble-top table in front of the main altar is where, since 1955, St Francis Xavier's remains have been held during their exposition. The main *reredos* has four panels illustrating the life of St Catherine. There is also an **art gallery** ⓘ *Mon-Thu, Sat 0900-1230, Sun 0900-1030, closed during services, Rs 5.*

Around the cathedral

Southwest of the cathedral's front door are the ruins of the **Palace of the Inquisition**, where over 16,000 cases were heard between 1561 and 1774. The Inquisition was finally suppressed in 1814. Beneath the hall were dungeons. In Old Goa's heyday this was the town centre.

There are two churches and a museum in the same complex as the Cathedral. The **Church and Convent of St Francis of Assisi** is a broad vault of a church with two octagonal towers. The floor is paved with tombstones and on either side of the baroque high altar are paintings on wood depicting scenes from St Francis' life while the walls above have frescoes with floral designs. The original **Holy Spirit Church** in the Portuguese Gothic (manueline) style was begun by Franciscan friars in 1517; everything except the old doorway was replaced by the larger present structure in the 1660s (itself restored 1762-1765). The convent now houses the **Archaeological Museum and Portrait Gallery** ① *T0832-228 6133, 1000-1230, 1500-1830, Rs 5*, with sculptures pre-dating the Portuguese, many from the 12th-13th centuries when Goa was ruled by the Kadamba Dynasty. There are 'hero stones' commemorating naval battles, and 'sati stones' marking the practice of widow burning. There is also a rather fine collection of portraits of Portuguese governors upstairs that is revealing both for its charting of the evolution of court dress as well as the physical robustness of the governors inside. Some governors were remarkable for their sickly pallor, others for the sheer brevity of their tenure of office, which must have set the portrait painters something of a challenge. (The ASI booklet on the monuments, *Old Goa*, by S Rajagopalan, is available from the museum, Rs 10.)

To the west is **St Catherine's Chapel**. It was built at the gate of the old city on the orders of Albuquerque as an act of gratitude after the Portuguese defeat of the forces of Bijapur in 1510. The original mud and thatch church was soon replaced by a stone chapel which in 1534 became the cathedral (considerably renovated in 1952), remaining so until Sé Cathedral was built.

On the road towards the Mandovi, northeast from the cathedral compound, lies the **Arch of the Viceroys (Ribeira dos Viceroys)**, commemorating the centenary of Vasco da Gama's discovery of the sea route to India. It was built at the end of the 16th century by his great-grandson, Francisco da Gama, Goa's Viceroy from 1597 to 1600. Its laterite block structure is faced with green granite on the side approached from the river. This was the main gateway to the seat of power: on arrival by ship each new Viceroy would be handed the keys and enter through this ceremonial archway before taking office. The statue of Vasco da Gama above the arch was originally surmounted by a gilded statue of St Catherine, the patron saint of the city. Walking east towards the convent from the arch you pass the **Gate of the Fortress of the Adil Shahs**, probably built by Sabaji, the Maratha ruler of Goa before the Muslim conquest of 1471. The now-ruined palace was home to the Adil Shahi sultans of Bijapur who occupied Goa before the arrival of the Portuguese. It was the Palace of the Viceroys until 1554 after which it served as both the hall of trials for the Inquisition and to house prisoners.

A little further still stands the splendid, domed baroque **Convent and Church of St Cajetan (Caetano)**. Pope Urban III dispatched a band of Italian friars of the Theatine order to spread the Gospel to the Deccani Muslim city of Golconda near Hyderabad but they got a frosty reception so headed back west to settle in Goa. They acquired land around 1661 to build this church, which is shaped like a Greek cross and is partly modelled on St Peter's in Rome. It is the last domed church in Goa.

The crypt below the main altar, where the Italian friars were buried, has some sealed lead caskets that are supposed to contain the embalmed bodies of senior Portuguese officials who never returned home. Next door is the beautiful former convent building which is now a pastoral foundation (closed to the public).

On a hill a good way further east is the modest **Chapel of Our Lady of the Mount**, dating from 1510, which gives you a good idea of how the other churches here must originally have looked. It is a peaceful spot with excellent panoramic views across Old Goa, evocative of the turbulent past when Albuquerque and Adil Shah vied for control of the surrounding area. The altar gilding inside has been beautifully restored. In front of the main altar lies the body of architect Antonio Pereira whose burial slab requests the visitor to say an Ave Maria for his soul.

Holy Hill

Between the domineering central monuments of Old Goa's broad tree-lined centre and Panjim stand the cluster of churches of Holy Hill. The first building you reach (on your left) as you leave the central plaza is the **Church and Convent of St John of God**, built in 1685 and abandoned in 1835. The **Museum of Christian Art** ⓘ *Sun-Thu 1000-1700, Rs 5*, is to the right, with 150 items gathered from Goa's churches, convents and Christian homes to give a rich cross section of Indo-Portuguese sacred craft in wood, ivory, silver and gold.

Next door sits the **Convent of St Monica** (1607-1627), the first nunnery in India and the largest in Asia. A huge three-storey square building, with the church in the southern part, it was built around a sunken central courtyard containing a formal garden. At one time it was a royal monastery, but in 1964 it became a theological institute, the Mater Dei Institute for Nuns. It was here in 1936 that Bishop Dom Frei Miguel Rangel is believed to have had a vision of the Christ figure on the Miraculous Cross opening his eyes, his stigmata bleeding and his lips quivering as if to speak. The vision was repeated later that year in the presence of the Bishop, the Viceroy Dom Pedro de Silva and a large congregation.

It is well worth the effort of the hike, taking the left fork of the road, to reach the **Royal Chapel of St Anthony** (1543) – dedicated to Portugal's national saint and restored by its government in 1961 – and, opposite, the **Tower of St Augustine**. The Augustinians came to Goa in 1572; the church they immediately began, bar the belfry, now lies in ruins. It once boasted eight chapels, a convent and an excellent library and was enlarged to become one of the finest in the kingdom. It was finally abandoned in 1835 because of religious persecution. The vault collapsed in 1842, burying the image; the façade and main tower followed in 1931 and 1938. Only one of the original four towers survives. The large bell now hangs in Panjim's Church of the Immaculate Conception. The Archaeological Survey of India is spearheading extensive repairs.

Behind is the **Chapel of Our Lady of the Rosary** (1526). Belonging to the earliest period of church building, it is called Manueline after Manuel I, the Portuguese king who oversaw a period of great prosperity that coincided with the country's conquest of Goa. The use of Hindu and Muslim craftsmen in building the chapel led to an architectural style that borrowed from Iberian decoration but also absorbed both local naturalistic motifs and Islamic elements (seen on the marble cenotaph). The church here has a two-storey entrance, a single tower and low flanking turrets. It was from here that Albuquerque directed the battle against the Adil Shahi forces in 1510.

Around Panjim

Gaspar Dias Fortress was finished around 1606. The Panjim-Ribandar causeway, built in 1634, gave it direct land access to the capital at Old Goa and its significance grew accordingly. The walls, likely laterite blocks 1.5 m thick and 5 m high, made space for 16 cannons. These saw repeated action against the Dutch until the middle of the 17th century, but the fortress' importance waned after the Maratha onslaught and it fell into disrepair under 15 years of occupation by a British garrison in the early 19th century. It was made new but the Portuguese army finally abandoned it in 1870 as a result of further damage sustained during the mutiny against the Prefect of 1835. For a while the military still stationed soldiers here to convalesce but by the 20th century it had crumbled beyond recognition. All that is left is one cannon at the Miramar circle that marks the possible site of the fort. **Miramar Beach** is a bit grubby but it's a pleasant drive with good views over the sea and, if you've got a little time to kill, it offers the best quick escape from the city.

The nearby fort **Cabo Raj Niwas** has fared little better: six cannons and some bits of wall crumbling in the gardens of Raj Bhavan, or the State Governor's House, are all that remain. It is closed to the public but you can get passes for Sunday Mass at 0930 on the gate. The first small **Our Lady of Cabo shrine** was built in 1541. Documents from 1633 refer to both the chapel and a fort with four guns. A British troops garrison stationed here from 1799 during the Napoleonic Wars explains the overgrown graves in the nearby **British Cemetery**. Around 1844, after the religious orders were abolished, the Archbishop of Goa was given the convent, which he converted into an impressive residence. It was the official address of the governor-general of Goa in 1918. Its grand interior was left intact after the Portuguese left in 1961. The viewing platform near the entrance gives superb views over the sweep of the coastline across the Mandovi estuary to Fort Aguada.

Panjim (Panaji) and Old Goa listings

For Sleeping and Eating price codes and other relevant information, see Essentials pages 15-18.

○ Sleeping

Panjim has a wide choice of accommodation, Old Goa none. There are upmarket options south of Panjim in the beach resorts of Miramar and Dona Paula, but for character it's best to book into one of the guesthouses in the atmospheric Fontainhas district. If you don't want to stay overnight you can pack the best of Panjim and Old Goa into a day. Guesthouses have early checkout to make way for new arrivals coming off the trains and buses.

Panjim *p34, map p36*
$$$$-$$$ Taj Vivanta, www.vivantabytaj. com. The Taj Vivanta opened in Panjim in 2009 and is a smart upmarket option centrally located. Common areas and restaurants are beautiful. Rooms are a little on the boutique-side, ie small and have this new trend of glass-walled bathrooms where you have to shut the blinds each time if you are sharing the room. Very odd. Overall everything you would expect from the Taj group.
$$$-$$ Mandovi, D B Marg, T0832-242 6270, www.hotelmandovigoa.com. Old building with hints of art deco, relaxing but

lacks great character. 66 large a/c rooms (river facing more expensive); rates include breakfast. 1st floor **Riorico** restaurant, popular pastry shop, terrace bar, exchange.
$$ Delmon, C de Albuquerque Rd, T0832-222 6846, www.alcongoa.com. 50 clean rooms, TV, desk, some a/c, breakfast included. Modern, comfortable hotel, popular restaurant.
$$ Manvins, 4th floor (accessed by lifts), Souza Towers, Muncipal Gardens/Church Sq, T0832-222 4412, www.goamanvins.com. 45 acceptable rooms with TV, some sleep 4, stunning views over Municipal Gardens and Mandovi River, hot water. Terrace has great views of Panjim. Unusual approach to interior design. Disco and pub.
$ Blessings, MG Rd, behind Bhatkar House, T0832-222 4770, hotelblessings@yahoo.com. 18 ordinary rooms, TV (extra Rs 50), 2 have huge terraces instead of balconies, restaurant, quiet tree-filled backyard.
$ Hotel Campal, opposite Kala Academy, Campal, T0832-222 4533. Clean rooms with TV and a/c possible, hidden in beautiful location in Campal area, near Kala Academy, Inox cinemas and the river.
$ Panjim Residency (GTDC), overlooking the river, T0832-242 4001. Best views from top floor, 40 good-sized rooms with balcony, some a/c (overpriced), good open-air

restaurant, often full, can organize tours and boat trips.

$ Rajdhani, Dr Atmaram Borkar Rd, T0832-222 5362. Modern business hotel with 35 smallish clean rooms with bath, some a/c (Rs 100 extra), pure vegetarian restaurant.

$ Virashree, opposite Mahalaxmi Temple, Dr Dada Vaidya Rd, T0832-222 6656, virashree @hotmail.com. 12 large, comfortable rooms with TV but lacking quality finish.

Fontainhas *p38, map p36*

$$$ The Panjim Peoples, opposite **Panjim Inn**, www.panjiminn.com. The latest heritage project from the Sukhija family, this one is genuinely top end with just 4 rooms, antique 4-poster beds and bathtubs, plus internet access. Changing art exhibitions on the ground floor.

$$ Panjim Inn, E212, 31 January Rd, T0832-222 6523, www.panjiminn.com. Goa's first heritage hotel is idiosyncratic, even in the context of the historic Fontainhas district. 14 rooms of varying size all fitted with 4-poster beds, a/c for an extra Rs 250.

$$ Panjim Pousada, up the road from **Panjim Inn**. Slightly cheaper sister hotel to the **Panjim Inn** with double rooms set around a permanent art gallery in a court-yard. It is an evocative, attractive renovation. Best rooms at the back overlook another courtyard. Recommended.

$ Afonso, near San Sebastian Chapel, Fontainhas, T0832-222 2359. Atmospheric family-run guesthouse, obliging and friendly, 8 clean rooms with bath, shaded roof terrace for breakfast. It's first come first served, though, as the owners don't take advance bookings. Recommended.

$ Comfort Guest House, 31 January Rd, T0832-222 8145. Good location, some rooms with TV, but often full and you can't book ahead. The cheaper of its 12 basic rooms have shared bath.

$ Pousada Guest House, Luis de Menezes Rd, T0832-561 8308. Pousada's basic rooms are higgledy-piggledy but have a/c, TV and fridge and attached bath. Will take advance bookings.

Around Panjim *p43*
Miramar Beach

$$$ Goa Marriott Resort, Mandovi River, T0832-246 3333, www.marriott.com. 153 large rooms, good facilities, pool, close to public beach, best hotel in area. Weekend buffet lunches popular with Panjim locals.

$$ Swimsea Beach Resort, T0832-246 4481, swimsea@satyam.net.in. 28 a/c rooms with small balconies, pretty underwhelming, sea-facing best, pool, if you want a quality beach experience better to stay elsewhere.

❷ Eating

Panjim *p34, map p36*

$$ Horseshoe, Rua de Ourem, T0832-243 1788, Mon-Sat 1200-1430, 1900-1030. Portuguese/Goan restaurant set in 2 high-ceilinged rooms with exceptionally good service. Most meals excellent value (Rs 60-80) but daily fish specials are far more costly (from Rs 300). The house pudding, a cashew cake, *Bolo San Rival* (Rs 50), trumps all the great main courses.

$$ Quarterdeck, next to Betim ferry jetty, T0832-243 2905. Goan, Indian, Chinese. Riverside location is the best in Panjim, very pleasant in the evening when brightly lit cruise boats glide gaudily by. Live music.

$$ Venite, 31 Janeiro Rd, T0832-222 5537, Mon-Sat 0800-2200, closes in the afternoon. The most charming of Panjim's eateries has 1st-floor balconies overlooking the Sao Thome street life and good music. Specializing in fish, this place has a great atmosphere.

$$ Viva Panjim, house no 178, signposted from 31 Janeiro Rd, T0832-242 2405. This family-run joint in the atmospheric Fontainhas quarter spills out of the restaurant and out into a courtyard, and dishes up Goan specials like *xacuti* and *cafreal* along with seafood, plus takeaway parcels of Indian, Chinese and continental.

$ Anandashram, opposite **Venite**
31 Janeiro Rd. Serving up platters of fish and veg thali, this is a great place to break *pao* (local bread) with the locals. Recommended.
$ Café Tato, off east side of Church Sq. Closed evenings. Something of a local institution, tiny little **Tato** is packed at lunchtime when office workers descend for its limited range of Goan vegetarian food. Expect tiny platters of chickpea, tomato or mushroom bhaji served with fresh puffed *puris* or soft bread rolls, or vegetarian cutlets and *thalis*. Upstairs is a/c.
$ Kamat, south end of Municipal Gardens. Pure vegetarian canteen, huge servings of *thalis*, excellent paper *dosas* and *puri bhajis*. Very popular large central dining hall.
$ Satkar, 18 June Rd, oppsote Bombay Bazaar. **Satkar** serves up fantastic pure veg food that runs the gamut from South Indian *idlis* and *thalis* to north Indian *sabzi* and tandoor dishes, and the best Punjabi samosas in India. Recommended.

Bakeries, cafés and snacks
$$ Pastelaria, Dr Dada Vaidya Rd. Good choice of cakes, pastries and breads. **Mandovi Hotel** has a branch too (side entrance).

🎵 Bars and clubs

Panjim *p34, map p36*
You can't go 20 paces in Panjim without finding a bar: pokey little rooms with a handful of formica tables and chairs and some snacks being fried up in the corner. Many are clustered around Fontainhas. The *feni* (Goa's cashew- or coconut-extracted moonshine) comes delivered in jerry cans, making it cheaper than restaurants. Try **Café Moderna**, near Cine National, food none too good, claustrophobic upstairs dining area, quality atmosphere.

🎭 Entertainment

Panjim *p34, map p36*
Read the 'today's events' columns in the local papers for concerts and performances.
Astronomical Observatory, 7th floor, Junta House, 18th June Rd (entrance in Vivekananda Rd). Open 14 Nov-31 May, 1900-2100, in clear weather. Rooftop 6-inch Newtonian reflector telescope and binoculars. Worth a visit on a moonless night, and for views over Panjim at sunset.
Inox, Campal, near Kala Academy, www.inox movies.com. Fantastic state-of-the-art glass-fronted cinema – like going to the movies in California. You can catch the latest Bolly- and Hollywood blockbusters here, and they try to show the Oscar-nominated Best Movies every year.
Kala Academy, D B Marg, Campal, T0832-222 3288. This modern and architecturally impressive centre designed by Charles Correa was set up to preserve and promote the cultural heritage of Goa. There are exhibition galleries, a library and comfortable indoor and outdoor auditoria. Art exhibitions, theatre and music programmes (from contemporary pop and jazz to Indian classical) are held, mostly during the winter months. There are also courses on music and dance.
MV Caravela, Fisheries dept building, D B Marg, Panjim, www.casinocity.com/ in/panjim/caravela. India's first floating casino is docked on the Mandovi, 66 m of high-rupee-rolling catamaran casino, all plush wall-to-wall carpets, chandeliers and sari-bedecked croupiers. The boat accommodates 300 people, has a sun deck, swimming pool and restaurant and the Rs 1200 entrance includes short eats and dinner and booze from 1730 till the morning.

Panjim *p34, map p36*
Feb/Mar In addition to the major festivals in Feb, the **Mardi Gras Carnival** (3 days preceding Lent in Feb/Mar) is a Mediterranean-style riot of merrymaking, marked by feasting, colourful processions and floats down streets: it kicks off near the Secretariat at midday. One of the best bits is the red-and-black dance held in the cordoned-off square outside the old world Clube Nacional on the evening of the last day: everyone dresses up (some cross-dressing), almost everyone knows each other, and there's lots of old-fashioned slow-dancing to curiously Country and Western-infused live music. The red and black theme is strictly enforced.

Mar-Apr Shigmotsav is a spring festival held at full moon (celebrated as **Holi** elsewhere in India); colourful float processions through the streets often display mythological scenes accompanied by plenty of music on drums and cymbals.

1st Sun after Easter Feast of Jesus of Nazareth. Procession of All Saints in Goa Velha, on the Mon of Holy Week.

Dec/Jan Fontainhas Festival of Arts. Timed to coincide with the film festival (see below), 30 heritage homes open up as temporary art and artefact galleries in an event organized by Fundacao Oriente, Goa Heritage Action Group and the Entertainment Society of Goa. International Film Festival of India, www.iffigoa.org. India's answer to Cannes: a 10-day film mart packed with screenings for the industry and general public alike, with its headquarters based around the Kala Academy and the Inox building on the banks of the Mandovi. Held in Goa since 2004. Food and Culture Festival at Miramar Beach.

8 Dec Feast of Our Lady of the Immaculate Conception. A big fair is held in the streets around Church Sq and a firework display is put on in front of the church each night of the week before the feast (at 1930). After morning Mass on the Sun, the Virgin is carried in a procession through the town centre.

24 Dec Christmas Eve. This is celebrated with midnight Mass at 140 churches in the state, but some of the best attended are the Church of the Immaculate Conception and Dom Bosco Church in Panjim and the Basilica of Bom Jesus in Old Goa.

○ Shopping

Panjim *p34, map p36*
Books and music
Broadway Books, next to Rock and Raaga off 18th June Rd, T0832-664 7038. Largest bookshop in Goa with good range.
Mandovi Hotel (see Sleeping). The hotel bookshop has a small range of books and magazines, including American news magazines.
Pedro Fernandes & Co, Rua Jose de Costa, near Head Post Office, T0832-222 6642. If you have a hankering to pick up a sitar or learn to play tabla, this small store has a great selection of musical instruments.
Varsha, near Azad Maidan. Holds a large stock in tiny premises, and is especially good for books on Goa. Obscure titles are not displayed but ask the knowledgeable staff.

Clothes and textiles
Government handicrafts shops are at the tourist hotels and the Interstate Terminus. There are other emporia on RS Rd.
Bombay Store, Casa Mendes, SV Rd, opposite Old Passport Office. A new branch of the lifestyle retail store has arrived in Goa close to the main shopping road 18th June Rd , with good selection of fabrics and clothes, as well as cards, stationery and homewares.
Fab India, Braganza Bungalow, opposite Indoor Stadium, Campal, T0832-246 3096. This is a particularly lovely branch of this great chain which sells handblock print clothes, textiles home furnishings and furniture. They have an extensive collection.

Government Emporia, RS Rd. Good value for fixed-rate clothes, fabric and handicrafts.
Khadi Showroom, Municipal (Communidade) Building, Church Sq, good value for fixed-rate clothes, fabric and handicrafts. Nehru jackets, Rs 250, plus perishables like honey and pickles.
Sacha's Shop, Casa Mendes, next to Bombay Store, T0832-222 2035. Dubbed a 'curious little space' by the owner, the eponymous Sacha, it is a collection of clothes, flea market finds, designer frocks, organic soaps and textiles.
Velha Goa Galeria, 4/191 Rua De Ourem, Fontainhas, T0832-242 6628. Hand-painted ceramics, wall hangings and tabletops of tiles.
Wendell Rodricks Design Space, 158 Luis Gomes Garden, Altinho, T0832-223 8177. Rodricks is probably Goa's most famous fashion designer who built his name making minimalist clothing. Here you'll find his luxury clothes and footwear.

▲ Activities and tours

Panjim *p34, map p36*
Cruises
Lots of evening cruises go along the Mandovi River, but as all boats seem to sport loud sound systems it's hardly a peaceful cruise.

Music lessons
Manab Das plays regularly at the **Kala Academy** and the **Kerkar** in Calangute (see page 52). He and his wife, Dr Rupasree Das, offer sitar and singing lessons to more long-term visitors. To arrange lessons T0832-242 1086 or email manabrupasreegoa@yahoo.in.

Tour operators
Alpha Holidays, 407-409 Dempo Tower, 4th floor, 16 EDC Patto Plaza, T0832-243 7450, www.alphagoa.com.
Pepper Tours, 127 Subash Chandra Bose Rd, Jawahar Nagar, Kadavanthara, PO Cochin 682020, T484-405 8886, T(0)9847-322802 (mob), www.peppertours.com.

⊖ Transport

Panjim *p34, map p36*
Air The airport is at Dabolim. From Dabolim airport, 29 km via the Zuari Bridge from Panjim, internal flights can be taken through **Air India** to **Mumbai** and **Thiruvananthapuram**. For pre-paid taxis, see box, page 10.

Airline offices Air India, 18th June Rd, T0832-243 1101. **Indian Airlines and Alliance Air**, Dempo House, D B Marg, T0832-223 7821, reservations 1000-1300, 1400-1600, airport T0832-254 0788, flights to **Bengaluru (Bangalore)**, **Delhi** and **Mumbai** daily (US$95), and **Chennai**. British Airways, 2 Excelsior Chambers, opposite Mangaldeep, MG Rd, T0832-222 4573. **Jet Airways**, Sesa Ghor, 7-9 Patto Plaza, T0832-243 1472, airport T0832-251 0354. Flights to **Mumbai** (US$103), and **Bengaluru (Bangalore)**. Kuwait Airways, 2 Jesuit House, Dr DR de Souza Rd, Municipal Garden Sq, T0832-222 4612. Sahara, Live-In Appt, Gen Bernard Guedes Rd, airport office, T0832-254 0043. To **Mumbai**, US$95, daily, and **Delhi**.
Auto-rickshaw Easily available but agree a price beforehand (Rs 20-35), more after dark. Motorcycle taxis and private taxis are a little cheaper.

Bus Local: Crowded **Kadamba (KTC)** buses and private buses operate from the bus stand in Patto to the east of town, across the Ourem Creek, T0832-222 2634. Booking 0800-1100, 1400-1630. The timetable is not strictly observed: buses leave when full. Frequent service to **Calangute** 35 mins, Rs 7; **Mapusa** 15 mins, Rs 8 (try to catch a direct one). Via Cortalim (Zuari bridge) to **Margao** 1 hr, Rs 10; **Vasco** 1 hr, Rs 8. To **Old Goa** (every 10 mins) 20 mins, Rs 5, continues to **Ponda** 1 hr, Rs 8.
Long distance: 'Luxury' buses and 'Sleepers' (bunks are shared). Prices double at Diwali, Christmas and New Year, and

during the May school holidays. Private operators: include **Laxmi Motors**, near Customs House, T0832-222 5745; company at Cardozo Building near KTC Bus Stand; **Paulo Tours**, Hotel Fidalgo, T0832-222 6291.

State buses are run by **Kadamba TC**, **Karnataka RTC**, **Maharashtra RTC**. Check times and book in advance at Kadamba Bus Stand. Unlicensed operators use poorly maintained, overcrowded buses; check out beforehand.

Buses to **Bengaluru** (**Bangalore**): 1530-1800 (13 hrs), Rs 300; **Belgaum**: 0630-1300 (5 hrs); **Gokarna** and **Hospet** (**Hampi**): 0915-1030 (10 hrs), Rs 150 (Rs 350 sleeper); **Hubli**: many; **Londa**: 4 hrs, Rs 60; **Mangalore**: 0615-2030 (10 hrs), Rs 180; **Miraj**: 1030 (10 hrs); **Mumbai**: 1530-1700 (15 hrs+), Rs 550 (sleeper), others (some a/c) Rs 300-450; **Pune**: 0615-1900 (12 hrs), Rs 200, sleeper Rs 400.

Car hire Hertz, T0832-222 3998; **Joey's**, town centre opposite the Mandovi Hotel, T0832-242 2050. **Sai Service**, 36/1 Alto Porvorim, north of the Mandovi Bridge, T0832-241 7063, or at airport. **Wheels**, T0832-222 4304, airport, T0832-251 2138.

Ferry Flat-bottomed ferries charge a nominal fee to take passengers (and usually vehicles) when rivers are not bridged. **Panjim-Betim** (the Nehru bridge over the Mandovi supplements the ferry); **Old Goa-Diwar Island**; **Ribandar-Chorao** for Salim Ali Bird Sanctuary.

Taxi Tourist taxis are white; hire from **Goa Tourism**, Trionora Apts, T0832-222 3396, about Rs 700 per day (80 km). Share-taxis run on certain routes; available near the the ferry wharves, main hotels and market places (up to 5). **Mapusa** from Panjim, around Rs 10 each. **Airport**, about 40 mins; Rs 380.

Train Some **Konkan Railway** trains stop at **Karmali**, T0832-228 6398, near Old Goa (20 mins taxi). **Rail Bookings**, Kadamba Bus Station, 1st floor, T0832-243 5054, 0930-1300 and 1430-1700. **South Central Railway** serves the Vasco-Londa/Belgaum line; for details see page 34, and Margao (Madgaon), page 104.

see page 34, and Margao (Madgaon), page 104.

Directory

Panjim *p34, map p36*
Banks Many private agencies change TCs and cash. **Thomas Cook**, 8 Alcon Chambers, D B Marg, T0832-243 1732, Mon-Sat. Also for Thomas Cook drafts, money transfers; **Amex**, at Menezes Air Travel, Rua de Ourem, but does not cash TCs. Cash against certain credit cards from **Central Bank**, Nizari Bhavan; **Andhra Bank**, Dr Atmaram Borkar Rd, opposite EDC House, T0832-222 3513; **Bank of Baroda**, Azad Maidan; **HDFC**, 18 June Rd, T0832-242 1922, 24-hr ATM, most convenient way to obtain cash in Panjim. **Embassies and consulates** Germany, Hon Consul, c/o Cosme Matias Menezes Group, Rua de Ourem, T0832-222 3261; Portugal, LIC Bldg, Patto, T0832-222 4233; UK, room 302, 3rd floor, Manguirish Bldg, 18th June Rd, T0832-222 8571, bcagoa@goa1.dot.net. **Internet** Among many charging Rs 35-40 per hr: **little.dot.com cyber café**, 1st floor, Padmavati Towers, 18th June Rd, 0930-2300. Best in town: **Suraj Business Centre**, 5 terminals upstairs, excellent fast connection (128 kbps ISDN line), 0900-2300. **Medical services** Goa Medical College, Av PC Lopez, west end of town, T0832-222 3026, is very busy; newer College at Bambolim; **CMM Poly Clinic**, Altinho, T0832-222 5918. **Post** Old Tobacco Exchange, St Thome, towards Old Patto Bridge, with Poste Restante on left as you enter, Mon-Sat 0930-1730, closed 1300-1400.

North Goa

While Baga and Calangute, the fishing villages first settled by the 'freaks', now stand as cautionary tales to all that's worst about mass tourism, Anjuna, a place synonymous with psychedelia, drugs and Goa trance parties, has managed to retain a village feel despite the existence of its unquestionably shady underbelly. It's a more tranquil place to be now that a 2200 music curfew has put a stop to outdoor parties. The weekly flea market is a brilliant bazar – like Camden or Portobello but with sacred cows, sadhus, fakirs and snake charmers – and makes it onto every holidaymaker's itinerary. But if you stick around you'll find that the little stretch of shoreline from the northern end of Anjuna Beach to the Chapora River is beautifully desolate: rust-coloured rugged cliffs covered with scrub interrupt scrappy bays strewn with laterite boulders. Pretty cliff-backed Vagator stands just south of the romantic ruins of Chapora Fort, with its busy fishing jetty, where trawler landings are met by a welcoming committee of kites, gulls and herons wheeling hungrily on high, while further upstream around the pretty village of Siolim young men wade through mangrove swamps to sift the muds for clams, mussels and oysters. Over the Chapora lies Arambol, a warm, hippy backpacker hamlet, and its beach satellites of Mandrem, Asvem and Keri and the wonderful little Catholic enclave clustered around the ancient Tiracol Fort.

Baga to Candolim → *For listings, see pages 62-83.*

The faultless fawn shoreline of Bardez *taluka*, particularly Calangute, until 40 years ago was a string of fishing villages. Now it acts as sandpit to the bulk of Goa's travel trade. Chock full of accommodation, eateries, travel agents, money changers, beggars and under-dressed, over-sunned charter tourists, the roads snarl up with minivans, buses and bikes, and unchecked development has made for a largely concrete conurbation of breezeblock hotels and mini markets. For all that, if you squint hard or come in monsoon you can still see what once made it such a hippy magnet: wonderful coconut-fringed sands backed by plump dunes occasionally broken by rocky headlands and coves. The main reason to head this way is for business, banks, or posh food and nightlife. To get out again, you can paddle in the waters of the Arabian Sea all the way between the forts of Aguada and Vagator.

Ins and outs

Getting there The NH17 acts as the main arterial road between all of Goa's coastal belt. From Panjim, the highway crosses the Mandovi Bridge to the area's main hub, Calangute (16 km from Panjim, 10 km from Mapusa). Buses from Mapusa (20 minutes) and Panjim (35 minutes) arrive at Calangute Bus Stand near the market; a few continue to Baga to the north from the crossroads. You can charter tourist minivans from places such as Panjim and Dabolim. The closest stop on the Konkan Railway route between Mumbai and Mangalore is Tivim near Mapusa. On market days there are boats between Baga and Anjuna. There are buses from Mapusa and Panjim to Calangute, Anjuna, Chapora and Arambol.

Getting around There are 9 km of uninterrupted beach between Fort Aguada and the bridge over Baga river in the north, which takes you to Anjuna. These are split into four beaches, south to north: Sinquerim, Candolim, Calangute and Baga. Each has its own stab at a high street, Calangute's being the most built up. There are taxis, motorcycle taxis, tourist vans and old Ambassador cabs, or cheap but slow public buses. Roads are fairly good for motorbikes and scooters; watch out for speed bumps. Accidents happen with grim regularity, but bikes give you the independence to zip between beaches.

Background

The name Bardez may have come from the term *bara desh* (12 'divisions of land'), which refers to the 12 Brahmin villages that once dominated the region. Another explanation is that it refers to 12 *zagors* celebrated to ward off evil. Or it could be *bahir des*, meaning 'outside land' – ie, the land beyond the Mandovi River. It was occupied by the Portuguese as part of their original conquest, and bears the greatest direct imprint of their Christianizing influence.

Calangute

More than 25 years of package tourism has guaranteed that there is little left to draw you to Calangute apart from ATMs, some decent restaurants and a quirky hexagonal *barbeiria* (barber's shop) at the northern roundabout. In the 1960s, the village was short-hand for the alternative life, but the main feature of the streets today is their messy Indian take on beach commercialism. Shops peddle everything from cheap ethnic tat to extravagant precious gemstones. The shacks on the beach serve good food and cheap beer and most fly the St George's Cross in tribute to Calangute's charter coin. Between the busy beachfront and the grubby main road, coconut trees give shade to village houses, some of which rent out private rooms.

Away from the town centre, the striking gold and white **Church of St Alex** is a good example of rococo decoration in Goa, while the false dome of the central façade is an 18th-century architectural development. The pulpit and the *reredos* are particularly fine. **Kerkar Art Complex** ① *Gaurawaddo, T0832-227 6017, www.subodhkerkar.com*, is a beautiful art space showcasing Subodh Kerkar's paintings and installation work. Inspired by the ocean, nature is both the theme and medium of his work, using shells, light and water to create static waves or, in his recent installations, using fishermen standing on the beach to create the shapes and forms of fishing boats – all captured in stunning black and white photography.

Calangute

Calangute map

To Baga
Casa Goa
Our Lady of Piety
COBRAVADDO
Arabian Sea
Tibetan Market
To Mapusa (6 km)
Nikki's
St John's
Football Pitch
Tibetan Market
Heritage Kathakali Theatre
SBI
BoB
UMTAVADDO
Menezes Supermarket
CALANGUTE
To Panjim
St Anthony's
GAURAVADDO
Kerkar Art Complex
Day Tripper
Literati
To Acron Arcade, Candolim (1 km), Sinquerim (3 km) & Aguada Fort (4 km)
N
200 metres
200 yards

Sleeping
Aashyana Lakhanpal 2
Coco Banana 4
Golden Eye 10
Kerkar Retreat 3
Martin's Guest Rooms 13
Pousada Tauma 17
Saahil 1
Villa Goesa 20

Eating
A Reverie 3
Bomras 1
Infanteria 2
Le Restaurant Français 4
Oriental at Hotel Mira 14
Plantain Leaf 7
Souza Lobo 8
Tibetan Kitchen 5

Baga

Baga is basically Calangute North: there's continuity in congestion, shops, shacks and sun loungers. Here though, there are also paddy marshes, water tanks and salt pans, the beach is still clean, and the river that divides this commercial strip of sand from Anjuna in the north also brings fishermen pulling in their catch at dawn, and casting their nets at dusk. The north bank, or **Baga River**, is all thick woods, mangroves and birdlife; it has quite a different, more villagey feel, with a few classy European restaurants looking out across the river. You can take an hour to wade across the river at low tide, then walk over the crest of the hill and down into Anjuna South, or detour inland to reach the bridge.

Candolim and Sinquerim beaches

The wide unsheltered stretch of beach here, backed by scrub-covered dunes, offers unusual visual stimulus courtesy of the unlovely rusting wreck of the *Sea Princess* tanker, an eyesore and environmental nightmare (the currents eddying around its bows are playing havoc with coastal sand deposition) which has been resting offshore for years waiting for someone to muster the will to remove it. Nevertheless, the beach still attracts a fair crowd: more staid than Baga and Calangute to the north, chiefly because its restaurants and hotels are pricier and the average holidaymaker more senior. The road from Calangute to Fort Aguada is lined with shiny glass-fronted shops, while the sands at the foot of the Taj complex offers the full gamut of watersports – jet skis, windsurfers, catamaran and dinghies are all for hire – making it a favourite of India's fun-loving domestic tourists.

Fort Aguada

The Portuguese colonizer's strongest coastal fort was built on this northern tip of the Mandovi estuary in 1612 with one goal: to stay the Dutch navy. Two hundred guns were stationed here along with two magazines, four barracks, several residences for officers and two prisons. It was against the Marathas, though, rather than the Dutch, that Aguada saw repeated action – Goans fleeing the onslaught at Bardez took refuge here – and its ramparts proved time and again impregnable. The main fortifications (laterite walls nearly 5 m high and 1.3 m thick) are still intact, and the buildings at sea level now house Goa's Central Jail, whose 142 male and 25 female inmates are incarcerated in what must be one of the world's prettiest lock-ups.

Reis Magos, the Nerul River and Coco Beach

The position of **Reis Magos**, across the Mandovi River from Panjim, made it imperative for Albuquerque to station troops on this shoulder of headland from day one of Portuguese rule – today, come for the views to the capital, and for the crumbling **Royal Fort** whose angular 16th-century architecture is now overrun with jungle. Its canons served as the second line of defence against the Dutch after Aguada. The next door **church** is where the village gets its name – this was where the first Mass on Goan soil was celebrated in 1550, and the Hindu temple was promptly turned over to a church to the three Magi Kings – Gaspar, Melchior and Balthazar – whose stories are told on the inside *reredos*. Fort Aguada and Fort Reis Magos are divided by the Nerul River: stop off at Nerul's **Coco Beach** for lunch and a swim. The temple in the village dates from 1910 and the Church of Our Lady of Remedies from 1569.

Baga

To Anjuna (2 km)

To Anjuna (500m)

Arabian Sea

St Ann's

Salt Lake

Salt Pans

Baga River

Baga Bridge

Football Pitch

BAGA

Lady of Candelaria

Natural Health Centre

Tito's Rd

Bike Hire

To Calangute

N

200 metres
200 yards

Sleeping
Alidia Beach Cottages 1
Baga Queen Beach Resort 2
Cavala 6
Nani's & Rani's 8
Riverside 3

Eating
Baba Au Rhum 2
Britto's 15
Casa Portuguesa 12
Fiesta 1
J&A's Italiano House 6
Le Poisson Rouge 11
Lila's Café 9

Bars & clubs
Mambo's 13
Sunset 10
Tito's 16

The trance dance experience

The 'freaks' (beatniks with super-nomadic genes, giant drug habits and names like Eight Finger Eddie) first shipped into Goa shortly after the Portuguese left. Some brought guitars on which, after soaking up a bit of Hindu spirituality on the way, they were charged with playing devotional songs at beach campfire parties.

By the end of the 1960s, thousands of freaks were swarming into Goa, often spilling down from Kathmandu, and word got back to proper paid-up acid rock musicians about the scene. Some more substantial entertainment was called for.

The first music to run through the speakers was rock and reggae. Led Zeppelin, The Who and George Harrison rocked up and played live, but the freaks' entertainment was mostly recorded: Santana, Rolling Stones and Bob Marley. Kraftwerk and synth had filtered in by the late 1970s but the shift to electronica only really came in the early 1980s when musicians got bored of the lyrics and blanked out all the words on albums of industrial noise, rock and disco, using the fully lo-fi production method of taping between two cassette decks. Depeche Mode and New Order albums were stripped down for their drum and synth layers. Some of the rock faithful were angry with the change in the soundtrack to their lives; at those early 1980s parties, when the psychedelic-meets-machine-drum sound that still defines Goa trance was first being pumped out, legend has it that the decks had to be flanked by bouncers.

The music, developing in tandem to German nosebleed techno and UK acid house, locked into a worldwide tapestry of druggy drumscapes, but the Goan climate created its own sound. As records would warp in India's high temperatures, music had to be put down on DATS rather than vinyl which in turn meant tracks were played out in full, unmixed. A track had to be interesting enough then, self-contained, so it could be played uninterrupted in full; producers had to pay more attention to intros, middles and outros – in short, the music had to have a story. It also meant there was less art to a set by a trance DJ in Goa than DJs in Manchester, Detroit and Paris, who could splice records together to make their own new hybrid sounds.

Many of the original makers of this music had absorbed a fair whack of psychedelia and had added the inevitable layer of sadhu thinking to this – superficially measured in incense, *oms*, dreads and the swirling dayglo mandalas that unmistakeably mark out a Goa trance party. The music reflected this: sitars noodled alongside sequencer music to make the Goan signature sound.

By the 1990s, though, Ecstasy had arrived in Goa. The whole party scene opened right up, peopled by Spiral Tribe crusties as well as middle-class gap year lovelies and global party scenesters who came looking for an alternative to the more mainstream fare in Ibiza. Paul Oakenfold's Perfecto was a key label in fuelling the sound's popularity but there were more: Dragonfly, The Infinity Project, Return to the Source. Today the music comes from labels like Electrojump, Hux Flux, Errorhead, Color Drop, Wizzy Noise, Psycho+ Trolls, Droidsect, Parasense, Peace Data, In-R-Voice. Although much of it is from European or Japanese studios, there's the odd label that's more homegrown, like the resolutely Goan label Made In Chapora.

Mapusa → *For listings, see pages 62-83.*

Standing in the nape of one of Goa's east–west ridges lies Bardez's administrative headquarters: a buzzy, unruly market town filled with 1960s low-rise buildings set on former marshland on the banks of the Mapusa River; (Maha apsa' means 'great swamps, a reference to Mapusa's watery past). Mapusa town won't find its way onto many tourist postcards, but it's friendly, small and messy, is an important transport hub and has an excellent daily **municipal market**, worth journeying inland for, especially on its busiest day, Friday. Open from early morning Monday to Saturday, it peters out 1200-1500, then gathers steam again till night, and has giant rings of *chourica* sausage, tumbles of spices and rows of squatting fruit and vegetable hawkers.

Walk east for the small 16th-century **St Jerome's Church**, or 'Milagres', Our Lady of Miracles (1594), rebuilt first in 1674 then again in 1839 after a candle sparked a devastating fire. In 1961 the roof was badly damaged when the Portuguese blew up a nearby bridge in their struggle with the liberating Indian army. The church has a scrolled gable, balconied windows in the façade, a belfry at the rear and an interesting slatted wood ceiling. The main altar is to Our Lady, and on either side are St John and St Jerome: the *retables* (shelves behind the altar) were brought from Daugim. The church is sacred to Hindus as well as Catholics, not only because it stands near the site of the Shanteri Temple but also because 'Our Lady of Miracles' was one of seven Hindu sisters converted to Christianity. Her lotus pattern gold necklace (kept under lock and key) may also have been taken from a Hindu deity who preceded her.

The **Maruti Temple** ① *west of the market opposite taxi stand*, was built on the site of a firecracker shop where Rama followers in the 1840s would gather in clandestine worship of first a picture, then a silver image, of monkey god Hanuman after the Portuguese destroyed the local Hindu temples.

Barely 5 km east of Mapusa lies **Moira**, deep in the belly of a rich agricultural district that was once the scene of Portuguese mass baptisms. The town is ancient – some say it was the site of a sixth or seventh century AD Mauryan settlement – and until the arrival of the Portuguese it must have been a Brahmin village. A total of seven important temples were destroyed during the Inquisition and six idols moved to Mulgaon in Bicholim district (immediately east).

Today the village is dominated by the unusual **Church of Our Lady of the Immaculate Conception**. Originally built of mud and thatch in 1619, it was rebuilt during the 19th century with square towers close to the false dome. The balustrades at the top of the first and second floors run the length of the building and the central doorways of the ground and first floors have Islamic-looking trefoil arches that contrast with the Romanesque flanking arches. There is an interesting exterior pulpit. Inside, the image of the crucifixion is unusual in having its feet nailed apart instead of together. A Siva *lingam* recycled here as the base of the font after its temple was razed is now in the Archaeological Museum at Old Goa. Moira's famous long red bananas (grown nearby) are not eaten raw but come cooked with sugar and coconuts as the cavity-speeding sweet *figada*.

Anjuna and around → *For listings, see pages 62-83.*

When the freaks waded across the Baga River after the squares got hip to Calangute, Anjuna was where they washed up. The village still plays host to a large alternative community: some from that first generation of hippies, but the latest influx of spiritual Westerners has brought both an enterprising spirit and often young families, meaning there's fresh pasta, gnocci, marinated tofu or chocolate brownies to be had, cool homespun threads to buy, great, creative childcare, amazing tattoo artists, alternative therapists and world-class yoga teachers. For the beautiful life lived cheap Anjuna is still hard to beat; the countryside here is hilly and lush and jungly, the beaches good for swimming and seldom crowded. A state crackdown has made for a hiatus in the parties for which Anjuna was once synonymous, but as you head south along the shore the beach shack soundtracks get progressively more hardcore, until **Curlies**, where you'll still find arm-pumping techno and trance.

Anjuna

Arabian Sea

To Ozran Beach
To ⑨, Vagator & Chapora
Oxford Arcade
Bungee Jump ⑧
⑥
SORANTOVADDO
⑤ BoB
②⑩
ANJUNA
⑫
MONTEIROVADDO
Artjuna
④
⑤
⑱
⑲
⑦
Flea Market Ⓜ
㉑
⑧
DANDOVADDO
③①⑰
Happy Hours Paragliding
To Baga & Calangute (500m)
To ②④⑦⑨ Ingo's Night Bazar, Brahmani Yoga, Arpora & Mapsa
Orchard Stores

N

200 metres
200 yards

Sleeping 🛏
Banyan Soul 1
Bougainvillea/Granpa's 9
Laguna Anjuna 3
Martha's Breakfast Home 5
Nilaya Hermitage Bhati 4
Red Cab Inn 6
Relddes Guest House 8
Rene's Guest House 12
Saiprasad Guest House 10

Tamarind 2
Yoga Magic Canvas Ecotel 7

Eating 🍴
German Bakery 21
Jam Connection 4
Joe Bananas 1
Om Made Café 2
Orange Boom 18

Shore 19
Xavier's 17

Bars & clubs 🍸
Curlys 3
Hilltop 9
Lilliput 7
Paradiso 8
Shiva Valley 11

The **Flea Market** ⓘ *Dandovaddo, south Anjuna, Oct-Apr Wed 0800 till sunset, water taxis or shared taxis from anywhere in Goa*, is a brilliant hullabaloo with 2000 stalls hawking everything from Gujarati wooden printing blocks to Bhutanese silver and even Burberry-check pashminas. The trade is so lucrative by the subcontinent's standards that for six months a year several thousand Rajasthani, Gujaratis, Karnatakans and Tibetans decamp from their home states to tout their wares. The flea had very different origins, and was once an intra-community car boot-style bric-a-brac sale for the freaks. Anjuna's links with trade pre-date the hippies though – the port was an important Arab trading post in the 10th and 12th centuries.

Saturday Night Bazar ⓘ *Arpora Hill, 1630-2400*, is a more sanitized and less headlong version of the flea. There's no shortage of dazzling stall fronts draped with glittering saris and the beautiful Rajasthani fare, but while there are fewer stalls there's more variety here; expats who've crafted everything from baby maharaja outfits and designer mosquito nets to handmade leather goods are more likely to pitch up here than at the Wednesday event. But there's no need to shop at all – the live music and huge range of food stalls make the Night Bazaar the weekly social event for tourist and long-stayer alike. You'll find most of North Goa out for the evening, and many businesses shut up shop for the night as a result of the bazar's magnetic appeal. Bring cash and an appetite.

The Anjuna area is also home to two of Goa's best contemporary yoga schools. **Brahmani** ⓘ *www.brahmaniyoga.com*, housed in two airy *shalas* in the gardens of Hotel Bougainvillea, runs workshops and drop-in classes, from excellent *ashtanga*, Mysore-style, to more experimental forms of yoga, like *Kundalini*, dance yoga, and *Scaravelli*. Packages with unlimited yoga are offered, but accommodation is not on site or specifically for yoga students. Ten minutes away in the neighbouring village of **Assagao**, the **Purple Valley Yoga Retreat** ⓘ *T0832-226 8364, www.yogagoa.com, US$600 per room per week including yoga and meals (see box, page 79)*, runs two-week *ashtanga* retreats with leading teachers like Sharath Rangaswamy, grandson of Sri K Pattabhi Jois, David Swenson and Nancy Gilgoff, two of the first to introduce *ashtanga* to the West in the 1970s. Lessons are held in a lovely *shala* in delightful gardens, food is vegetarian and the atmosphere collegiate.

Vagator

Vagator's beaches are possibly Goa's most dramatic: here, muddied sand bays upset by slabs of gray rock, quite different from the bubblings of porous laterite in Anjuna, fall at the bottom of terraced red cliffs planted with coconut trees that lean out towards the crashing waves, some of their trunks painted bright neon from past parties.

Big Vagator Beach is a long sweep of beach to the right of the main access road, behind which stands the profile of the wide outer rim of the ruined **Chapora Fort** against a stunning backdrop of India's western coastline, stretching beyond Goa's northern borders and into Maharashtra. The factory you can just pick out in the distance marks the border.

To your left, running inland, is **Little Vagator Beach**, its terracing lorded over by **Nine Bar**, a giant venue with an unswerving musical loyalty to trance (see page 74). Just out of sight is **Ozran Beach**, christened 'Spaghetti Beach' by English settlers for its Italian community. Though a bit scrappy and dogged by persistent sarong sellers, **Spaghetti** is more sheltered, more scenic and more remote than the other beaches, ending in tumbled rocks and jungle, with excellent swimming spots. To get straight to Spaghetti from Vagator follow the signposts to Leoney Resorts, then when you reach the headland turn off the tarmac road onto one of the gravel tracks following the sign for Shiva Place shack; coming from Anjuna, take the path that starts just inland from Zoori's and thread your way down the gravelly terracing.

Chapora Fort

Looming over the north end of Big Vagator Beach, there's little left of Chapora Fort but crumbling blocks of black rock overgrown with tawny grasses and a general air of tranquil ruination. Built by Adil Shah (hence the name, Shah pura), the remaining ramparts lead out to a jutting promontory that affords spectacular sunset views across the mouth of the Chapora River, where fishing boats edge slowly out of harbour and seabird flocks settle on the sand spits across from Morjim.

Chapora village itself may be too feral for some tastes. At dusk the smoke from domestic fires spreads a haze through the jungle canopy between which Portuguese houses stand worn and derelict. Down by the river's edge men lean to mend their fuzzy nets while village boys saunter out to bat on threshed fields, and Enfields and Hondas hum along the potholed roads bearing long-stayers and Goan village folk home – many of them toting fresh catch from the buzzing fish market (ignore the stern 'No Entry' signs and ride on in) held every sunset at the harbour. Along the village's main street the shady bars are decked with fairy lights and the internationals (who call Chapora both 'home' and, in an affectionate nod to its less savoury side, 'the Bronx') settle down to nurse their drinks.

The flat arc of the estuary here is perfect for cycling: the rim-side road will take you all the way out to the bridge at **Siolim** where you can loop back to take a look at the **Church of St Anthony**. Built in 1606, it replaced an earlier Franciscan church dating from 1568. Both Goa's Hindu and Catholic communities pray to St Anthony, Portugal's patron saint, in the hope of good fishing catches. The high, flat-ceilinged church has a narrow balustraded gallery and Belgian glass chandeliers, with statues of Jesus and St Anthony in the gabled west end.

Splendid Portuguese houses stand scattered about the village's shadows in varying degrees of disrepair; it's worth walking around to take in some of the facades. You can even stay in one which has been refurbished, the lovely Siolim House, see page 66. The ferry that once crossed the Chapora River at the northern end of the village no longer runs (there's a bridge instead) but it's worth heading up this way for the little daily fish market and the handful of food stalls selling fresh grilled catch. The village also has a basic bar, **Mandola**, on the coast road heading back towards Chapora, selling European snacks and cold beer.

Arambol, Keri, Morjim, Asvem, Mandrem → For listings, see pages 62-83.

The long bridge that spans the Chapora River joins Bardez to the last – and thus most heavily Hindu – of the new conquests, hilly Pernem *taluka*. This is the gateway to a series of pretty and quiet beaches that hug the coastal road in a nearly unbroken strip up to the Maharashtra border, where a tiny pocket of Catholicism squats in the shadow of the pretty pride of the district, Tiracol Church and Fort. Haphazard and hippy Arambol has a warm community feel and is rightly popular with open-minded travellers of all ages, who are drawn to its vibey scene, its live music, the dolphins that fin along its beaches and its famous saltwater lake. Sunset takes on the magnitude of a ritual in Arambol: people gather to sing, dance, juggle, do *capoeira* or find a silent spot for meditation and contemplation. To the south, Mandrem and Asvem are more chic and less busy, and will suit those less prepared to compromise on their accommodation. With construction of a new airport near Pernem and a large road bridge over the Tiracol to Maharashtra in the offing, Northern Goa will become more accessible, and there will be increased development no doubt.

Ins and outs
All of Pernem *taluka* is within easy reach of the hotels in Panjim or Calangute, but you'd be doing yourself a disservice to visit what are arguably North Goa's loveliest beaches just on a day trip. Better to set up camp in one and make it your base to explore the rest. If you are crossing the bridge at Siolim on a motorbike turn left off the new main road immediately after the bridge to use the smaller, more scenic coastal roads. There also regular buses to the villages from Mapusa and from Chopdem. Each beach is about 10 minutes apart.

History
The Bhonsles of Sawantwadi in modern Maharashtra were the last to rule Pernem before being ousted by the Portuguese in 1788, and Maratha influences here remain strong.

Arambol Beach

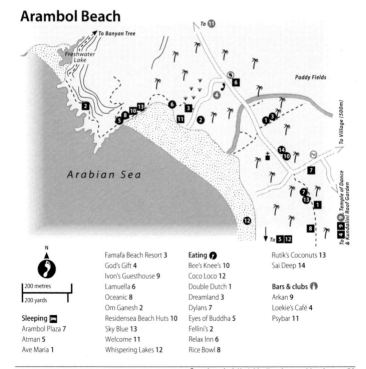

	Famafa Beach Resort 3	**Eating**
	God's Gift 4	Bee's Knee's 10
N	Ivon's Guesthouse 9	Coco Loco 12
	Lamuella 6	Double Dutch 1
200 metres	Oceanic 8	Dreamland 3
200 yards	Om Ganesh 2	Dylans 7
	Residensea Beach Huts 10	Eyes of Buddha 5
Sleeping	Sky Blue 13	Fellini's 2
Arambol Plaza 7	Welcome 11	Relax Inn 6
Atman 5	Whispering Lakes 12	Rice Bowl 8
Ave Maria 1		

Rutik's Coconuts 13
Sai Deep 14

Bars & clubs
Arkan 9
Loekie's Café 4
Psybar 11

Arambol (Harmal)

Arambol, which you reach when the plateau road noses down through paddy fields and cashew trees, is a beautiful long stretch of sand at the bottom of a bumpy dirt track that's fringed with stalls selling brightly coloured, heavily embroidered clothes and pretty *lungis*. This is the creative and holistic hub of Goa – many Western designers, artists, performers, yogis and healers have been inspired to make the area home, and because people have put down roots here, the village is abuzz with industriousness. Flyers advertise *satsang* with smiling Western gurus: there's also *tabla* classes and drumming circles, yoga teacher training, reiki and belly dancing. Arrive at the right time of year and you might catch the International Juggling Convention in full swing, or stumble across a phenomenal fire-dancing show by performers who work their magic on the stages of Vegas. Arambol is also synonymous with live music, with everything from Indian classical to open mike, Sufi musicians and psychedelic metal bands playing in rotation at the beach bars. Inevitably, though, Arambol's ever-growing popularity means both long and short-term accommodation get more expensive by the year.

You have to skirt the beach's northern cliff and tiny basalt rocky bays by foot to reach the real lure: a second bay cut off from the roads and a **natural 'sweet water' lake** that collects at the base of a jungle spring. The lagoon collects just metres from the high tide line where the lush forest crawls down to the water's edge. You can walk up the spring's path to reach a belt of natural mineral clay: an idyllic spot for self-service **mud baths**. Further into the jungle is the famous **banyan tree**, its branches straddling 50 m, which has long been a point of Hindu and hippy pilgrimage. Or clamber over the boulders at the north to join the scrappy dirt track over the headland for the half-hour walk it takes to reach the achingly lovely and reliably empty **Keri Beach**.

Keri (Querim) and Tiracol Fort

Goa's northernmost beach is uniquely untouched. The drive towards Keri (Querim) along the banks of the Tiracol River from Pernem passes through some stunning rural areas untouched by any tourist development.

Walk across deep dunes to a casuarina thicket and out onto empty sand that stretches all the way from the mouth of the Tiracol river to the highland that splits it from Arambol. There's just one solitary shack at either end of the beach, both of which can arrange rooms with villagers from Rs 100. **Querim** gets busy on weekends and is now host to the parties that have been forced on from Anjuna, but remains a lovely spot of sand. You can reach the beach from the north on foot from the Tiracol ferry terminal, or from the south by walking round the headland from Arambol. The Tiracol ferry runs every 30 minutes 0600-2130 taking 15 minutes, depending on the tides. If you arrive outside these times you can charter a fishing boat for Rs 55.

Tiracol (Terekhol), at the northernmost tip of Goa, is a tiny enclave of just 350 Catholics on the Maharashtra border just 3.5 km across where *feni* production is the biggest business. Its name probably comes from *tir-khol* ('steep river bank') and it's a jungly little patch of land full of cashew trees, banyans, orange blossoms, black-faced monkeys and squirrels.

The small but strategic **fort** ① *0900-1800, cross Tiracol river by ferry (every 30 mins 0600-2130) and walk the remaining 2 km; ferries take cars and motorbikes*, stands above the village on the north side of the Tiracol River estuary on a rugged promontory with amazing views across the water. Its high battlement walls are clearly visible from the

Arambol headland. Built by the Maharaja Khem Sawant Bhonsle in the 17th century, it is protected from attacks from the sea, while the walls on the land side rise from a dry moat. It was captured in 1746 by the Portuguese Viceroy Dom Pedro Miguel de Almeida (Marques de Alorna), who renamed it Holy Trinity and had a chapel built inside (now St Anthony's). You can explore the fort's battlements and tiny circular turrets that scarcely seem fit for slaying the enemy. The views south are magnificent. Steps lead down to a terrace on the south side while the north has an open plateau.

St Anthony's Church ⓘ *open on Wed and Sun for Mass at 1730*, inside the tiny fort, was built in the early 1750s soon after the Portuguese takeover. It has a classic Goan façade and is just large enough to cater for the small village. In the small courtyard, paved with laterite blocks, stands a modern statue of Christ. The **Festival of St Anthony** is held here at the beginning of May (usually on the second Tuesday) instead of on the conventional festival day of 13 June.

Morjim (Morji) to Asvem

Morjim, which stands on the opposite side of the estuary from Chapora, has two wide sweeping beaches that both sit at the bottom of separate dead end streets. This inaccessibility means that, development-wise, it has got away relatively unscathed. The southern, protected, turtle beach appears at the end of the narrow track that winds along the north bank of the Chapora rivermouth. Loungers, which are mostly empty, are strewn haphazardly north of the official-looking **Turtle Nesting Control Room**.

The wide shoreline with its gentle incline (the water is hip height for about 100 m) is washed by easy rolling breakers, making it one of North Goa's best swimming beaches. The northern beach, or **Little Morjim**, a left turn off the main coast road is, by comparison, an established tourist hamlet with guesthouses and beach huts. Plans for an upmarket hotel complex here with a private beach, which would deny local people free access to a section of the waterfront, have been dropped, so this fine stretch of beach should be safe.

The road from Morjim cuts inland over the low wooded hills running parallel to the coast. After a few kilometres the road drops down to the coast and runs along the edge of northeast tilting **Asvem Beach**. (Morjim faces Chapora to the south and west.) The northern end of this peaceful palm-fringed beach is divided by a small river.

Mandrem

Mandrem creek forces the road to feed inland where it passes through a small commercial centre with a few shops and a bank. Mandrem village has the **Shri Bhumika Temple** housing an ancient image. In the **Shri Purchevo Ravalnatha Temple** there is a particularly striking medieval image of the half-eagle, half-human Garuda, who acts as the *vahana* (carrier) of Vishnu.

A little further on, a lane off to the left leads down towards the main beach and a secluded hamlet in a beautifully shaded setting. The **beach** is one of the least developed along this stretch of coast; for the moment it is managing to tread that fine line between having enough facilities for comfort and enough isolation to guarantee idyllic peace. Further north there is a lagoon fringed by palm trees and some simple rooms, virtually all with sea view.

North Goa listings

For Sleeping and Eating price codes and other relevant information, see Essentials pages 15-18.

● Sleeping

For more on places to stay in this area, see www.goatourism.org/accomodation/north.

Calangute *p51, map p52*

$$$$ Pousada Tauma, Porba Vaddo Calangute, T0832-227 9061, www.pousada-tauma.com. A shady little complex built of Goa's trademark laterite rock set around a beautiful pool. It's discreet but full of character, with old-fashioned but under-stated service. Suites are spacious, but come with shower not bath. Classy without a modern 5-star swagger.

$$$ Kerkar Retreat, Gauravaddo, T0832-227 6017, www.subodhkerkar.com/retreat. Get inspired by staying above this beautiful art gallery (see page 52). Subodh Kerkar is a visionary artist and has created a beautiful oasis in the midst of Calangute. Just 5 doubles with an overflowing library and naturally an array of stunning artwork. A guesthouse feel that's ideal for families since it also has a kitchen you can use. Somewhat sedate by Calangute's standards – but that's a compliment. Highly recommended.

$$$-$$ Villa Goesa, Cobravaddo, off Baga Rd, T0832-227 7535, www.nivalink.com/vilagoesa. 57 clean rooms, some a/c, some very shaded, excellent restaurant, lovely gardens, pool, quiet, relaxing, very friendly owners, 300-m walk from the beach. Recommended.

$$$-$ Golden Eye, Philip's Cottages, Gauravaddo, T0832-329 0549, www.hotel goldeneye.com. 25 roomy suites and clean rooms, all with balcony, a/c or non a/c, half-price singles, right on the beach (built before restrictions) with genuine sea views.

$$-$ Coco Banana, 5/139A Umtavaddo, back from Calangute Beach, T/F0832-227 6478, www.cocobananagoa.com. In a nice neighbourhood in the backlanes of Calangute, this is one of the best local guesthouses and has 6 spotless en suite bungalows set in a leafy garden. All rooms come with nets and fridges, some have TV and a/c, and the place is airy, light and comfortable. The Swiss-German owners are caring and helpful. They also rent out 2 apartments in **Casa Leyla**, and have a whole house, **Soledad**, with all mod cons and maid service.

$ Martin's Guest Rooms, Baga Rd, T0832-227 7306, martins@goatelecom.com. 5 rooms in family house, attractive verandas, use of kitchen but on the busy main road and could do with a lick of paint.

$ Saahil, Khobra Vaddo, Baga Rd, T0832-227 6647. Lots of big, clean rooms within walking distance of all the action. Good value.

Baga *p52, map p53*

Of the family guesthouses on the northern side of Baga River up towards Arpora, those to the left of the bridge (west or seaward) are quieter. You might be able to get a room in houses/cottages with good weekly or monthly rates. Standards vary so check room and security first. Try Wilson Fernandes at **Nani's & Rani's** or ask at **Four Seasons Restaurant** at Jack's Corner.

$$$-$ Cavala, Sauntavaddo, top end of Baga village, T0832-227 6090, www.cavala.com. Sandwiched between Baga Rd and a big field stretching towards the mountains, **Cavala** is traditional but very well maintained, with friendly and attentive management, and set in lovely gardens. The 30 rooms are big, with giant fridges and huge bathrooms, although only shower. Some have TV. Recommended.

$$ Alidia Beach Cottages, behind the Church, Sauntavaddo, T0832-227 9014, alidia@rediffmail.com. Weave around the pot-plant covered yards to reach this charming hotel in a series of 2-storey cottages, run professionally but with the warmth of a guesthouse. Rooms are spotless and old fashioned, with features including handmade fitted wardrobes, and offer lots of privacy around the well-tended garden. New pool. One of the best of its kind so book ahead.

$$-$ Riverside, Baga River by the bridge, T0832-227 7337, www.hotelriversidegoa.com. Nice location overlooking the river. Clean modern rooms with good balconies. Some cottages with kitchens available near the pool. Has a tour group feel about the place, but lovely location.

$ Baga Queen Beach Resort, T0832-227 6880. Close to beach, better value than others nearby, 15 good-sized, clean rooms with bath.

$ Nani's & Rani's, T0832-227 7014, www.naniranigoa.com. 8 spartan rooms (shared or own bath), budget meals served in pleasant garden, bar, email, STD/ISD. One of the few local budget options with a sea view and a relaxing quiet location – attractive main building. Renowned healer Dr Patrick hosts sessions and workshops here on occasion. Short walk across Baga Bridge for nightlife.

Candolim and Sinquerim beaches *p52*
$$$$ Fort Aguada Beach Resort, Sinquerim, T0832-664 5858, www.tajhotels.com. The self-confessed sprawling Taj complex spreads over 36 ha. In descending order of cost, these are 17 hilltop family villas that make up the Aguada Hermitage, 130 rooms with sea views at the Fort Aguada Beach Resort, built in the fort's ruins, and scores of cottages for up to 8 on the beach in the **Taj Holiday Village**. The complex has many 5-star facilities including 2 freshwater pools, 9 restaurants, Ayurvedic and other spa treatments, plus golf, tennis and a creche. The Thai restaurant on site is recommended.

$$$$-$$$ Aashyana Lakhanpal, Escrivao Vaddo, Candolim, T0832-248 9225, www.aashyanalakhalpal.com. One of the most stunning places in Goa – beautiful gardens with great swathes of green lead right down to the beach. If you don't fancy

the beach, there's a lovely pool. And the rooms and villas are beautifully decorated. This is a great place to hide away.

$$$$-$$$ Lemon Tree Amarante Beach Resort, Vadi, Candolim, T0832-398 8188, www.lemontreehotels.com. Try to get one of the 6 heritage rooms here, housed inside a grand century-old Portuguese mansion but restored now, as the rest of the hotel, in mock 15th-century Portuguese style. The complex has Wi-Fi, a kids' centre, pool, 2 restaurants, a spa and all mod cons.

$$$$-$$$ The Sol, road opposite Bank of India, Nerul (directly inland 2 km from Calangute/Sinquerim), T0832-671 4141, www.thesol.in. Designed by fashion designer Tarun Tahiliani this is a nouveau heritage-style property where they strive to create an atmosphere that honours Goa as it once was. Tucked in lush foliage with views of Sinquerim river, the rooms are big, the beds are 4-postered, but it does seem a bit new and not quite as polished as it should.

$$$ Marbella Tourist Home, left off the road to Taj Fort Aguada Beach Resort, T0832-247 9551, www.marbellagoa.com. Splendid mock-Portuguese period mansion with 6 lovingly decorated rooms. Its owners have scavenged bona fide antiques and furnishings like mosaic tiles from old villas to create this elegant and unpretentious homestay in a forest at the end of a dirt track. Lovely garden sit-out for meals. All rooms have a/c and cable TV.

$ Ludovici Tourist Home, Dando, Sinquerim, T0832-237 9684. Pretty family home set back off the main road with 4 modest en suite doubles, all with fan. It very much feels that you are one of the family. There's a bar and restaurant and a lovely porch with chairs that gives onto a spacious garden. Sedate and modest guesthouse with traditional charm.

Mapusa and inland *p55*
$$$$ Panchavatti Corjuem, on the island of Corjuem, 9 km east of Mapusa, T(0)9822-

580632, www.islaingoa.com. Just 4 elegant rooms in this stunning secluded house overlooking the Mapusa River, potentially by time of reading there will be more rooms available in neighbouring properties. Not much to do here except laze in bliss with Ayurvedic massages and facials, amazing food and mesmerizing views.

$$$ Presa di Goa, near Sublime, Arais Wado, Nagoa-Saligao, T0832-240 9067, www.presadigoa.com. Dubbed as a country house retreat, **Presa di Goa** is a beautifully decorated place with antique furniture, some with 4-poster beds. There's a relaxed vibe and a lovely swimming pool. And even though it's not close to the sea and there's not much going on around there, it's perfect for getting away from it all and it's walking distance to one of Goa's best restaurants, **Sublime**.

$$$ Wildernest, www.wildernestgoa.com. Amazing eco resort tucked into the border of Goa with Maharashtra and Karnataka – it's 1½ hrs from Mapusa. This eco-hotel sprung up as a protest – the land was to be sold to a big mining company and in order to save it **Wildernest** was created. So this place is the real deal, they are concerned with the local wildlife and there is a research centre on-site and for guests there are birdwatching tours and waterfall treks. The luxe log cabins hug the valley with amazing views of the ghats and there is an infinity swimming pool hanging just above the horizon. Working closely with 6 local villages from all three states, they offer up delicious home-cooked food. This is a totally alternative view of Goa. Whole-heartedly recommended.

Anjuna and around *p56, map p56*
At the budget end, the best options in Anjuna, Vagator and Chapora tend to be unofficial, privately owned residences.

$$$$ Nilaya Hermitage Bhati, T0832-227 6793, www.nilayahermitage.com. A luxury retreat in topaz on a hilltop in Arpora overlooking Anjuna. Elite accommodation in 10 unique bungalows and 4 tents in lush gardens set around a beautiful plunge pool. Tennis, badminton, gym, yoga, jogging trail, DVD library and excellent restaurant, highly prized music room, but some have found fault with the warmth of service and food.

$$$ Laguna Anjuna, Sorantovaddo, T(0)9822-162111, www.lagunaanjuna.com. Atmospheric cottages spiralling off behind stunning swimming pool and lush gardens, some with amazing domed ceilings and divan daybeds. Beautiful bathrooms and comfy beds. This is a vibey place serving up great food from the popular restaurant by the frangipani-fringed pool. The only drawback is the terracotta-tiled Goan roofs, they look pretty but you will hear your neighbours and it is a romantic place. You can come and use the lovely pool for Rs 150.

$$$-$ Hotel Bougainvillea/Granpa's, Gaumwadi, T0832-227 3270, www.goacom.org/hotels/granpas. Popular but pricey for what you get – better value elsewhere. Lovely pool though. More likely to attract yogis than the party crowd.

$$ The Banyan Soul, behind German Bakery, off Flea Market Rd, T(0)9820-707283, sumityardi@thebanyansoul.com. Chic complex of rooms nestled under giant banyan tree. Funky modern rooms with beautiful artistic lighting and all mod cons, sexy showers, TVs and compact verandas. The only drawback is the rooms take up the whole site; there are smart gardens bordering the hotel, but it is a bit boxed in.

$$ The Tamarind, 3 km inland from Anjuna, behind St Michael's Church, Kumar Vaddo, Mapusa Rd, T0832-227 4319, www.the tamarind.com. Great value. 22 rooms with flagstone floors and balconies in stone-built Portuguese-style house set in landscaped gardens with pool, which some complain fails to catch sunlight. Courtesy bus service to beaches.

$$ Yogamagic Canvas Ecotel, 2 km from Anjuna beach, T0832-652 3796, www.yogamagic.net. A luxury campsite in a field of paddy and palms featuring 7 Rajasthani hunting tents, a naturally filtered pool, immaculate gardens of bougainvillea, lilies and lotus flowers, yoga and holistic therapies, delicious vegetarian South Indian food and environmentalism. There are also eco-lodges, teepees and the Maharani suite, a wing of the main house with its own veranda. Solar panels, compost loos, 5 mins' walk from Brahmani yoga centre (page 57).

$$-$ Martha's Breakfast Home, House No 907, Monteiro Vaddo Anjuna, T0832-227 3365, mpd8650@hotmail.com. Set in the gardens of a house that give onto an orchard where pigs roam in the shade. 8 spic-and-span rooms, twin beds, small shower rooms (cold water) with nice little balconies. Better though are the 2 villas with 2 doubles, little lounges with telly, and kitchenettes with gas stove, sink and fridge. Ask for the Sunset Villa, which has incredible views. Basic but perfect.

$ Pebbles, Piqueno Peddem, Flea Market Rd, T(0)9923-649993, www.anjunapebbles.com. Well-located for market and beach – you could almost get away without getting your own transport which is a rarity for Anjuna. Basic rooms but great value, friendly owner. You might want to hide on Wed when the road will be busy outside.

$ Rene's Guest House, Monterio Waddo, opposite Artjuna, T0832-227 3405, renesguesthousegoa@yahoo.co.in. A gem: 14 rooms around a colourful garden run by a friendly family. Best are the 3 self-contained cottages, with 4-poster beds, good kitchens with gas stove, sinks and big fridges; these are meant for long lets (2 are designed for couples, the other sleeps 3). Individual rooms are decent too.

$ Saiprasad, north beach, T(0)9890-394839, saiprasadguesthouse@gmail.com. Uninspiring rooms some with a/c, but great location – right on the beach which is unusual for Anjuna. Pretty little gardens and beachside restaurant.

Vagator *p57*

$$$ Casa Vagator, Cliffside, T0832-227 4931, www.casaboutiquehotels.com. Chic branch of these boutique hotels with modern rooms, some of the deluxe ones are a bit over the top with beds on plinths. Beautiful pool area. Also owns **Casa Colvale** a stunning property on the River Chapora 15 mins' drive from Mapusa, T(0)9373-081973, www.casacolvale.com.

$$$ Living Room, T(0)9975-870846, www.livingroomhotel.in. Brand new shiny hotel in stark contrast to the rest of the Vagator abodes. Definitely a sign of the changing face of Goa, chic rooms with all the mod cons, nice courtyard pool, Arabian themed restaurant.

$$ Leoney Resort, 10-min walk from beach, T0832-227 3634, www.leoneyresort.com. 13 rooms, 3 cottages, a/c extra Rs 400. Clean, modern, family run, low-key, quiet, pool.

$$ Ocean Bliss, Ozran Beach, T0832-645 4563, oceanbliss_24@hotmail.com. Selection of bamboo cottages hanging on the cliffside, bit pricey but all with TV/fridges and great views.

$$-$ Julie Jolly, **Jolly Jolly Lester**, **Jolly Jolly Roma**, T0832-227 3357, www.hoteljollygoa. com. With 3 different properties offering a whole range of a/c and non-a/c rooms with hot showers, TV and a pool.

$ Garden Villa, Main Beach Rd, near **Abu John's**, T0832-652 9454. 8 clean rooms, some with bath, restaurant with a decent choice.

$ Paradise Huts, Small Vagator, Ozran, T(0)9922-230041. Good selection of huts on the cliff, some with views, shared bathroom.

$ Thalassa Huts, T(0)9850-033537. Tucked behind popular atmospheric restaurant, nice huts with attached bathrooms. Short walk down the cliff to the beach. Although staying here might affect your waistline.

Chapora Fort p58

Chapora Fort and Siolim caters mainly for long-term budget travellers.

$$$ Siolim House, opposite Vaddy Chapel, Siolim, T0832-227 2138, www.siolim house.com. Lovingly restored 300-year-old house. This is a stunning property once owned by the governor of Macau. 4-poster beds, epic bathrooms and fantastic large windows. Restored in 1999, it recently had a further facelift in 2009 and the pool is one of the most beautiful places you could find yourself. Great food, chilled atmosphere. There is a sister property with just 3 rooms away in another beautifully crafted house – **Little Siolim**. And further up on the Arpora Hill there is a new development for rent aimed at yoga groups. Highly recommended.

$ Noble Nest, opposite the Holy Cross Chapel, Chapora, T0832-227 4335. Basic but popular, 21 rooms, 2 with bath but ample facilities for sharing, exchange and internet.

Arambol p60, map p59

Arambol is low budget. Pack a sleepsheet and a lock (few rooms are secure but many have lockers).

$ Arambol Plaza, Beach Rd. Very different to the usual Arambol fare but lacking any design aesthetic, basic modern rooms with swimming pool.

$ Atman, Palm Grove Girkar waddo, next to Surf Club, T(0)9881-311643, www.atmangoa. com. A lovely collection of palm-fringed coco huts with good use of sari drapes and chic decor, all surrounding a pretty restaurant. There is also a yoga space and it's all just steps from the beach.

$ Ave Maria, inland, down track opposite police post, Modhlowado, T0832-224 7674, avemaria@satyam.net.in. One of the originals, offering some of the best accommodation. Simple but nevertheless recommended. Very popular.

$ Famafa Beach Resort, Beach Rd, Khalchawada, T0832-224 2516, famafa_in@ yahoo.com. 25 rooms in an unimaginative development on the right of the stall-studded road down to the beach. No a/c, but many pitch up for the hot showers.

$ God's Gift, House No 411, Girkar Waddo, T0832-224 2391. Budget-friendly family guesthouse a little way from village, but a nice walk through palm grove, with hammocks hanging about its balconies. Western loos, balconies and kitchenettes. Still plenty of restaurants around and close to Kundalini Yoga Roof Garden and Temple of Dance.

$ Ivon's Guest House, Girkarwada, near **Kundalini Yoga Roof Garden**, www.goa rambol.com. Popular rooms looking out on to the coconut grove, from the top floor you can just about see the sea. Basic clean rooms with attached bathrooms.

$ Lamuella, 292 Beach Rd, T0832-651 4563, lamuella@gmail.com. 1 floor of spotless and brilliantly maintained rooms sandwiched between the fantastic garden café and therapy treatment rooftop of **Lamuella**, Rooms are sweet and clean and have hot water. Great vibe here and good place to meet people.

$ Luciano Guest Rooms, Cliffside, T(0)9822-180215. Family house with toilet and shower. Cliffside rooms get heavily booked up.

$ Oceanic, inland at south end, T0832-224 2296. Secluded guesthouse with simple rooms, all hidden behind wall in mature gardens, popular. Recommended.

$ Om Ganesh, Cliffside on way to Sweet Lake, T0832-224 2957. Lots of rooms clustered on the cliffside – great views and lots of places to hang a hammock. Rooms are basic, but with attached bathroom. Ask at Om Ganesh restaurant on cliff or in town at Om Ganesh General Store. Now have rooms on high street above general store too. Recommended.

$ Residensea Beach Huts, north end of Arambol Beach, T0832-224 2413. Basic bamboo shacks set back from the beach in pretty location, all have fans and secure locker facilities (outside toilets). German Shepherd keeps watch.

$ Sky Blue, north end of beach, near Eyes of Buddha. 4 small rooms in a cottage, shared veranda, great beach view, usually taken by long-term visitors.

$ Whispering Lakes, Girkar Waddo, follow signs to Surf Club and Wooden Heritage, T(0)9272-462656, rajanbhai@gmail.com. Simple huts hugging lake, each with it's own cushioned sit-out hanging over the lake. A bit pricey for what you get and noise can carry from the Surf Club, but very pretty and unique location – catch special sunsets from your lakeside podium.

Keri and Tiracol Fort *p60*

Keri is pretty out of the way and it helps to have your own transport. The beaches around here are dotted with typical budget beach shacks.

$$$$ Fort Tiracol Heritage Hotel, Tiracol, T0236-622 7631, www.forttiracol.com. In 2003 the owners of **Nilaya** in Arpora, took over Fort Tiracol to create an outpost of isolated, personalized luxury with unbroken views of the Arabian Sea. Just 7 exquisite rooms, all with giant en suite, set in the fort walls that surround the Catholic Church which is still used by the 350 villagers of the wholly Christian Tiracol for their Mass. Goa's most romantic hotel. Prices include breakfast and delicious dinners. Highly recommended.

$ Dream House, Keri, off main road on way to beach, T(0)9604-800553. Large rooms with attached bathroom sandwiched between family house and **Coconut Inn** rooftop restaurant.

$ Raj Star, Keri, near New English High School, T(0)9881-654718, raj-star@hotmail.co.uk. Pretty rooms in attractive guest house. Nice communal sitting areas.

Morjim to Asvem *p61*

This pretty stretch of coastline is dominated by hotels and restaurants catering to Russian package tourists, with a few notable exceptions.

$$$ Ku, Asvem Beach, www.kugoamorjim.webs.com. In stark contrast to its new naff neighbour in Aswem, **Marbella Beach Resort**, Ku is quite possibly one of the most beautiful places you can stay in India. Dubbed a 'zen hotel in mother india' there are stunning handbuilt Japanese-style wooden bungalows with sliding doors and true rustic elegance. And sitting on the upper deck looking out at rice fields and palm trees or gazing down at the water feature that runs through Ku like an aorta, is pretty close to Nirvana. Problem is you just won't want to move out. Exceptional food too.

$$$ Sur La Mer, above Asvem Beach, T(0)9850-056742, www.surlamergoa.com. Beautiful rooms with 4-poster beds and super-stylish bathrooms around lovely pool. All have good views of the neighbouring fields and the beach; with special mention going to the stunning penthouse with almost 360-degree views of paradise. The food is also highly praised.

$$$ Yab Yum Eco Resort, Asvem Beach, T0832-651 0392, www.yabyumresorts.com. 10 deluxe 'eco-domes' made of local materials – blue painted lava rocks make up the bases, woven palm leaves and mango wood the roofs, spread across a huge shady expanse of coconut and banana grove tucked behind a row of trees from the sand dunes. The pods come in 2 sizes – family or single – but both have living areas, and en suite bathrooms. It's classy, discreet and bohemian. There's a reading room over the sea, a yoga *shala*, and a children's teepee crammed with toys. The price includes breakfast and papers. Also now new chic accommodation available at sister property in the hills, **Jivana Plantation**, which is absolutely stunning.

$$$-$$ Leela Cottages, Asvem Beach, T(0)9823-400055, www.leelacottage.com. Close to the beach, these are posh wooden huts with antique doors from a palace in Andhra Pradesh and decorated with beautiful furniture. Very stylish but with relaxed vibe and on-site yoga too.

$$$-$ Arabian Sea, Aswem Beach, past Aswem village, T0832-329 0703, www.meems beachresort.com. Range of accommodation, simple huts to pretty luxe wooden bungalows. Bit pricey but very popular.

$$ Aquatica, Asvem Beach, T(0)9096-620023, www.aquaticagoa.com. Cute cottages nestled at the bottom of the hill with beautiful restaurant and on-site pilates and yoga studio. Prices reflect the vibe of the area.

$$ Yoga Gypsys Asvem, close to Yab Yum, T(0)9326-130115, yogagypsys@yahoo.com. 5 terracotta bungalows, tree huts and tipis in a peaceful palm grove close to a Hindu temple the base for group yoga retreats but can also be rented independently. Teachers such as Katy Appleton and Scaravelli teachers Marc Woolford and Sophy Hoare have all flexed their toned bodies here. Check the website for coming attractions.

$$-$ Montego Bay Beach Village, Vithaldas Wado, Morjim, T(0)9822-150847, www.montegobaygoa.com. Rajasthani-style luxury tents pitched in the shade past beach shrubs at the southern end of the beach, plus log cabins, a/c rooms and a beach villa.

$ Palm Grove, Asvem towards Morjim, T(0)9657-063046, www.palmgrovein goa.com. Quirky place with cottages and huts named 'Happy Hippie' and 'Rosie Slow' there are comfy beds and a sweet beach restaurant.

Mandrem *p61*

$$$$ Elsewhere's Beach House, T(0)9326-020701, www.aseascape.com. 3 lovely bedrooms in the understated luxury of a redecorated 19th-century house on a sandy spit with the sea on one side and a saltwater creek the other. Living room, dining room and kitchen are sea facing; facilities include maid service, day and nightwatchman, stereo, extra for cook. Minimum rental period 1 week at US$2000-4000. Also runs the **Priest's Houses**, 3 similarly carefully restored villas nearby.

$$$$ Elsewhere Otter Creek Tents. Under same ownership as above, 3 luxury Rajasthani tents each with 4-poster beds, en suite hot showers, private jetties and sit-outs.

$$$ Mandala, next to Ashiyana, access from Aswem–Mandrem road, T(0)9657-898350, www.themandalagoa.com. The highlights at Mandala are the chic 2-storey hut extravaganzas – downstairs you will find a swing seat, up the stairs a tented bedroom with 2 loungers on the front deck. There are murals by a Danish artist Ulrik Schiodt. There are also stylish rooms in the main house and smaller huts.

$$$-$ Ashiyana, Mandrem River, opposite Villa River Cat by footbridge, www.ashiyana-yoga-goa.com. Spacious resort catering mainly to yoga fellows borrows from Bali and Morocco – dark wooden treehouses, beautiful rooms painted in aubergine, draping saris and magnificent handcrafted mosquito nets. The vibe is chilled and yogic, with a range of focused yoga retreats and holidays inviting people to dip in to yoga, dance and meditation. Beautiful restaurant on site and a chic café shack on the beach across the footbridge. Also a great spa with massages and treatments, and a pool on the way. Prices are per person and often rooms are shared.

$$-$ Villa River Cat, Junasvaddo, T0832-224 7928, www.villarivercat.com. 13 rooms in a 3-tiered roundhouse overlooking the river and a wade over deep sand dunes from the beach. The whole place is ringed with a belt of shared balconies and comes with big central courtyards stuffed with swings, sofas, plantation chairs and daybeds. There's a mosaic spiral staircase and a cavalier approach to colour: it's downbeat creative and popular with musicians and actors – in the best possible way. Cat lovers preferred.

$ Dunes, Junasvaddo, T0832-224 7219, www.dunesgoa.com. **Dunes** is just set back off the beach with lots of nice-sized coconut huts and a few bungalows, most with attached bathroom. A peaceful place to stay with a good restaurant that has occasional live music.

$ O'Saiba, Junasvaddo, T(0)9420-897906, sunnymehara@yahoo.com. **O'Saiba** offers a range of coco huts, bungalows and 2 small blocks of typical guesthouse rooms. Also has a good restaurant by the beach.

🍴 Eating

Even Calangute's most ardent detractors will brave a trip for its restaurants, some of which are world class. While costly by Indian standards a slap-up meal will cost you a fraction of its equivalent at European prices.

Calangute *p51, map p52*

$$$ A Reverie, next to **Hotel Goan Heritage**, Holiday St, T0832-317 4927, areverie@rediff mail.com. After a recent facelift, this chic restaurant is a great place to splash out.

$$$ Bomras, Candolim towards Sinquerim, T(0)9822-10 6236, bawmra@yahoo.com. Mouth-watering Burmese and Asian fusion food, such as seared rare tuna, mussel curry and Nobu-esque blackened miso cod. Fantastic vegetarian dishes and curries too. Washed down with quite possibly the best cocktail in the world spiced with lemongrass and ginger. Beautiful chic setting – amidst the bright lights of Candolim, you could almost blink and miss it.

$$$ Souza Lobo, on the beach. Somewhat of an institution, this place serves up excellent fresh seafood, lobster (Rs 550) and sizzlers served on a shaded terrace, well-known restaurant that has managed to retain a good reputation for years.

$$$ Sublime, H No 1/9-A, Grande Morod, Saligao, inland from Candolim, T(0)9822-484051. Worth driving inland, this is one of the best restaurants in Goa. Chris Saleem offers up fantastic fusion food using as much organic and locally sourced products as possible – ginger battered calamari with apricot chutney, fish in banana leaf,

asian-style beef and delicious desserts. It's a beautiful restaurant tucked away – it would be a secret if it wasn't so deservedly popular and now he has his own TV show too. Booking essential.

$$ Oriental, The Royal Thai Cuisine, **Hotel Mira**, Umtawaddo, T0832-329 2809, T(0)9822-121549. Impeccable Thai food in pretty courtyard in odd looking hotel. Home-made tofu daily, plus pasta, steaks, schnitzel, goulash, cakes and excellent espresso. Cookery courses Mon 1400-1700.

$ Café Ciocolatti, main road Candolim, T(0)9326-112006. Fantastic range of all things chocolate. Lovely daytime café.

$ Infanteria, Baga Rd, near beach roundabout. 'The breakfast place' to locals, Rs 125 set breakfast, eggs, coffee, juice, toast. Bakery and confectionery. Very atmospheric.

$ Plantain Leaf, near petrol pump, Almita III. T0832-227 6861. Mean *dosas*, jumbo *thalis*, sizzlers and a range of curries; unbeatable for your pukka pure vegetarian Indian.

$ The Tibetan Kitchen, at the bottom of a track leading off Calangute Beach Rd. 0900-1500, 1800-2230. This airy garden restaurant is part tent, part wicker awning, part open to the skies. Tibet's answer to ravioli – *momos* – are good here, but more adventurous starters like prawns, mushrooms and tomatoes seeping onto wilting lettuce leaves are exceptional.

Baga *p52, map p53*

$$$ Casa Portuguesa, Baga Rd. An institution of a restaurant run by German/Goan couple with live music in the gloriously overgrown jungle of a garden. Strongly recommended.

$$$ Fiesta, Tito's Lane, T0832-227 9894. Open for dinner Wed-Mon. One of Baga's destination eateries serving Mediterranean nosh in stylish surroundings, unusual Portuguese and Italian dishes, and great desserts. Even though it's a big restaurant, the tables seem spread out and hidden –

there is even one table inside an old fishing boat. Good for romantic dinners.

$$$ J&A's Ristorante Italiano House, 560 Baga River, T0832-228 2364, www.little italygoa.com. Open for dinner Oct-Apr. Jamshed and Ayesha Madon's operation – along with their pizzas and pastas – has earned them an evangelical following.

$$$ Le Poisson Rouge, next to Baga Bridge, Baga River, T0832-324 5800, www.lepoisson rouge-goa.com. Gregory Bazire is turning things French in Goa with this restaurant in Baga and Aquatica in Asvem. This is French fusion with a little Goa thrown in – fish, filet de boeuf and veggie options served up in all kinds of 'emulsions' and who can refuse a sweet samosa and ice cream for dessert.

$$ Britto's Bar and Restaurant, Baga Beach, T0832-227 7331. Cajie Britto's puddings are an institution and his staff (of 50) boast that in high season you'll be pushed to find an inch of table space from the restaurant's inside right out to the seashore. Great range of traditional Goan dishes like vindaloo and *cafreal*.

$ Baba au Rhum, off the main road between Arpora and Baga. Serving up fantastic cappuccino, breads, croissants and salads in a laid-back vibe. Extraordinarily good desserts, coffee éclair or chocolate and passion fruit pie anyone?

$ Lila's Café, north bank of Baga River, T0832-227 9843, lilacafe@sify.com. Closed evenings. Slick German-run restaurant, good selection of European dishes, check blackboard for specials, smoked kingfish. Home-made cheeses and jams. Also serves beers. Shaded terrace overlooking the river.

Mapusa *p55*

$ Ashok, opposite the market's entrance. Serves genuine South Indian breakfasts like *uttapam* and *dosa*.

$ Hotel Vilena, near Municipality building. Has 2 restaurants, 1 on the rooftop and 1 a/c indoors, best food in town.

$ Mahalaxmi, Anjuna Rd. A/c, South Indian vegetarian.

$ Navtara, on Calangute Rd. Excellent range of Goan, South and North Indian fare – great dosas and yummy mushroom xacuti with puris for breakfast.

Anjuna and around *p56, map p56*

$$$ Xavier's, Praias de San Miguel (follow signs from behind small chapel near flea market site, bring a torch at night), T0832-227 3402. One of the very first restaurants for foreigners has grown into a smart restaurant with 3 separate kitchens (Indian/Chinese/ continental), excellent fresh seafood, tucked away under palm trees.

$$ Blue Tao, Anjuna main road. Good range of salads, pizzas, tofu dishes and juices (including wheatgrass), also has a kids' area and puts on belly dancing and live music evenings.

$$ Joe Bananas, through the Flea Market behind Curlies, family-run place offering up amazing fish thalis – the fish is seasoned to perfection or there is a great array of bhaji like pumpkin.

$$ Shore Bar, 400 m north of flea market. Lovely raised beach bar and restaurant offering a prime spot for sunset. It used to be party central here back in the day, now the focus is on the food and the view. Great menu with lots of traditional Indian and Goan food, as well as some of the best salads in Goa – paneer and toasted cashews on a bed of greens, or an amazingly generous prawn version. Extensive wine list and creative cocktails.

$ German Bakery, south Anjuna, towards the Flea Market and **Curlies**. A little fiefdom of bohemian perfection: the bakery's sign is hung over a huge garden with an awning of thick tropical trees, where comfortable mattresses pad out the sides of low-slung booths. The atmosphere alone is habit-forming, but the food is the real thing too: huge salads with every healthy thing under the sun (including sprouts and avocado) plus good veggie burgers, Indian food and extreme juices. There is massage available on site and a small health food counter.

$ The Jam Connection, just off Baga shortcut road, South Anjuna. Thu-Tue 1100-1900. A family favourite for lazy lunches, or skip straight to dessert – there are 21 types of home-made ice creams, chocolate fondue, eclairs and profiteroles, while mains are mostly Mediterranean and Middle Eastern like quiches, salads, gazpacho, humous and tahini plates. Proper coffee.

$ Om Made Café, north beach Anjuna cliff, T(0)9823-850276. Another serving from the owner of Le Poisson Rouge, this chic little café has great coffee, tasty sandwiches, wraps and salads and great ice cream from amore. A welcome addition to the neighbourhood.

$ Orange Boom, south Anjuna, Flea Market Rd. Daytime only. Efficient and spotlessly clean canteen. Food is hyper-hygienic and meticulously made, with a menu offering the usual breakfast fare plus 100 ways with eggs (like poached eggs and French toast), most served with mushrooms and grilled tomatoes. Baked beans can be masala or Heinz (proper ketchup on the tables), also croque madame and sautéed avocado on toast.

Vagator *p57*

Several restaurants line the streets to the beach. Some serve good fresh fish including **Mahalaxmi**. **Primrose Café** serves tasty health foods and also hosts spontaneous parties.

$$$ Le Bluebird, T0832-227 3695. A short and excellent menu matched by an amazing wine list (Chablis, Sauterne, Sancerre) and fine cheeses in the garden restaurant of a long-standing reputation run by Goan/ French couple. Entrecôte and fillet are cooked in a variety of ways and sauces, and there's ratatouille and bouillabaisse, king and tiger prawns and lobster

$$ The Alcove, on the cliff above Little Vagator. Smartish, ideal position, excellent

food, pleasant ambience in the evening, sometimes live music.

$$ Bean Me Up, near the petrol pump, Vagator, T0832-227 3479. Closed all day Sat and daily 1600-1900. You can choose from salad plates and delicious tempeh and tofu platters. There's massage offered on site, a useful noticeboard for mind-body-spirit stuff, kids' area and a few simple, clean rooms for rent. Under new management, so maybe in for a revamp.

$$ Mango Tree, in the village. Wide choice of continental favourites.

$$ Thalassa, on the clifftop overlooking Ozran Beach, T(0)9850-033537. Beautiful restaurant perched on the cliff, amazing sunset views and great Greek food from dolmades and souvlaki to salads and moussaka. Booking essential. Great boutique on site too.

$ Fusion, on the clifftop above Ozran Beach. A sprawling tent strewn with cushions and low tables, offering beautiful sunset views through silhouettes of coconuts. Try spit-roasted chicken, humous, baba ghanoush, vegetable quiche, roast tatties or one of the dozens of salads (including beetroot, Caprese and carrot). More substantial stuff is mostly Italian: spaghetti, lasagne, meatballs, a great pizza list and for pudding, pannacotta, tiramisu and profiteroles. Lemonade recommended.

Chapora Fort *p58*

$$ Da Felice & Zeon, above **Babba's**. Open 1800-2400. Just a handful of tables dancing with fairy lights and psychedelic art at this rooftop restaurant run by the Italian brothers Felice and Zeon. Felice is an Italian chef in London over monsoon, Zeon makes trance music and trance art. Carbonara, lasagna, prosciutto, spaghetti alla vongole all feature, but meat is recommended.

$$ La Befa, Chapora Market road. Some people drive an hour for the roast beef sandwich here. Or there's parma ham or marinated aubergine – all on freshly baked French bread.

$ Jai Ganesh Juice Bar, the hub of Chapora. This is the only place to be seen in Chapora for every juice under the sun.

Arambol *p60, map p59*

There are beach cafés all along the main beach and around the headland to the north. The 2 German bakeries fall short of the lovely restaurant in Anjuna.

$$ Double Dutch, Beach Rd, T0832-652 5973, doubledutchgoa@yahoo.co.uk. 0700-2300. Lovely laid-back garden restaurant with sand underfoot and lots of leafy foliage and sculptures created by the owner around. Breakfasts are tip top here with home-made breads like carrot or watermelon seed and also home-made jams – you can also get a full 'English' Goa style. Candle-lit in the evening, there are lots of great salads as well as Dutch dishes, Indonesian, Thai, pastas and the steaks come with the best recommendation. There is a Sun morning second-hand market and a bit of live music too. Recommended.

$$ Fellini's, Beach Rd, T0832-229 2278, arambolfellini95@yahoo.com. Thu-Tue 1000-2300, Wed 1800-2300. Fellini's is an institution serving up pizzas and calzone to the hungry masses.

$$ Lamuella, Main Rd, T0832-651 4563. Atmospheric restaurant in the heart of Arambol under the watchful eye of chef Gome. Home-made mushroom or pak choi raviolis, great fish, tagines, salads and huge breakfast platters. This is a great spot to meet and greet. There's also a great shop specializing in clothes crafted by Westerners in Arambol. If you can't face the night market, see what Westerners get up to creatively here. Recommended.

$ Bee's Knees, Main Rd, nearish to Double Dutch. Great value with range of Mexican dishes, Indian and salads. Deservedly popular.

$ Dreamland Crepes, main road, near **Double Dutch**. Blink-and-you-miss-it 2-tier coffee house serving up fabulous cappuccinos and healthy juices, as well as a wide range of crêpes and sandwiches. And Wi-Fi.

$ Dylans, coconut grove near **Rutik's Coconuts** and behind **Coco Loco**. Coffee houses have sprung up in Arambol to fuel the creative types and designers that make Arambol their home. If you like your coffee strong, this Manali institution delivers, along with hot melty chocolate cookies and soups and sandwiches. Film nights and occasional live music.

$ Eyes Of Buddha, north end of Arambol Beach. Long on Arambol's catering scene, this place has you well looked after with scrupulously clean avocado salads, a great range of fish and the best Indian food in town, all topped off with a great view of the beach. Highly recommended.

$ Relax Inn, north end of beach. The only beach shack with a good reputation, this is a firm favourite with the expats. Slow service but worth the wait for *spaghetti a la vongole*, grilled kingfish with ratatouille and a range of fresh pasta dishes.

$ Rice Bowl, next door to **Eyes of Buddha**. Great views south across Arambol Beach, with a billiard table. Simple restaurant that has been serving reliably good Chinese for years. All the usual chop suey, wontons, noodles and sweet and sours of calamari, pork, beef or fish, plus Japanese dishes like *gyoza*, *sukiyaki*, tempura and Tibetan *momos*.

$ Rutik's Coconuts, entrance to beach behind **Coco Loco**. Serving up thalis all day, this place is best visited for coconuts. It's a great place to hang-out, see and be seen.

$ Sai Deep, Beach Rd. A family-run *dhaba* offering amazing veg and fish plates at lunchtime, mountainous fruit plates and a good range of Indian and continental food.

Morjim to Asvem *p61*

Join the masses as they descend on La Plage every Sun. Restaurants in Morjim central cater mainly to Russians.

There are plenty of shacks catering to Asvem and Mandrem beaches. Some have free loungers, others charge up to Rs 100.

$$$ Ku, Asvem, T(0)9326-123570, www.kugoamorjim.webs.com. Serving up fresh food that she fancies cooking each day, Maria runs a chic little ship here with tastes from the Mediterranean and from Asia. This is a special place – shhh don't tell everyone!

$$$ La Plage, Asvem, T(0)9822-121712. Hidden slightly from the beach, you can still feel the breeze in this lovely laid-back restaurant. The food is excellent and ambitious; tapas include beef carpaccio, chicken liver and fish ceviche, there's fish soup with aioli and *ile flottante* or everyone's favourite chocolat fondant for pudding. There are specials every day, as well as renowned rare tuna and wasabi mash and a giant hamburger. Vegetarians well catered for too, try the sage butter ravioli and the breakfasts are legendary. Nice wines, fabulous peppery Bloody Marys with mustard seeds and curry leaf. Also has rooms and an excellent shop featuring jewellery from expat designer Simona Bassi.

$ Arabian Sea, Asvem Beach. Tasty *thalis*, both Indian and Mediterranean and range of salads, fish and tofu dishes. Also has a good range of rooms and huts.

$ Change Your Mind, Asvem Beach. This typical beach shack serves up great Indian food, tasty fried calamari and monumental fruit plates. This is where the expats come to enjoy their day off.

$ Pink Orange, Asvem Beach. Low-level seating overlooking the beach with chilled out trance vibe. Menu serves up a great range of salads, sweet and savoury crêpes, juices, coffees and great choc brownies. Recommended.

Mandrem *p61*

$$ Café Nu, Junnaswaddo, Mandrem Beach. T(0)9850-658568. Another helping from Sublime guru Chris Saleem Agha Bee – great food in laid-back locale. Mustard encrusted fish, Asian beef and the mega salad is monumental. Good food to linger over. Highly recommended.

$ Dunes, Mandrem Beach. Great restaurant with the typical extensive and eclectic menu, but all done well. Very good Indian and fish dishes. Regular high-quality live music, great sound system.

$ Oasis, south end Mandrem Beach. Perched above Mandrem Beach, with good Indian food, pizzas and sunset views.

$ Well Garden Pizzeria, near O'Saiba, off main road. Sweet garden restaurant with great range of pizzas, broccoli and pesto pastas and an almost infamous warm chickoo cake. Service can be a bit hit or miss though.

Bars and clubs

Calangute *p51, map p52*
Saligao

Club WestEnd, near Porvorim, 3 km out of Calangute towards Panjim. Miles out of the way, this club gets away with hosting 3-day parties by being too remote to disturb anyone.

Baga *p52, map p53*

Locals know which way their bread is buttered, and in this neighbourhood, it's beer up. Many bars here have a happy hour from 1700 to 1930 and show live Premier League football, in a bit of a home-from-home for many visitors. Along the beach, shacks also serve a wide range of drinks and cocktails to sip while watching the sunset.

Cavala, Sauntavaddo, top end of Baga village. A genuine bar, with friendly atmosphere, attentive staff, great cocktails, and occasional live music evenings.

Sunset, north of Baga River. A great place to watch the goings-on of Baga Beach as dusk falls. Prime location but less hectic as it's north of the river bridge.

Tito's, Tito's Lane, T0832-227 5028, www.titosgoa.com. Tito's is an institution in Goa, and has adapted down the decades to reflect the state's changing tourist reality by going from a down-at-heel hippie playground in the 1960s to a swish international dance club and now the focus seems to be more on food – are the dancing days of Goa really over? Further along Tito's Lane towards the beach is the Tito's spin-off, **Mambo's**. It's more laid back than the club and free to get in.

Anjuna *p56, map p56*

The days of all-night parties in North Goa are long gone, and politicians imposed a ban on loud music after 2200 for several seasons – they keep changing the rules so sometimes you might be lucky and find yourself dancing until dawn . Indoor venues like **Liquid Sky** in Aswem and **West End** in Saligao stay open later. Wed and Fri tend to be the big nights especially at places like **Curlies**, but there is usually something going on each night over the Christmas and New Year period; just ask around (taxi drivers invariably know where). Venues are often recognizable by illuminated trees and luminous wall hangings.

Curlies, at the very far south of Anjuna. A kind of unofficial headquarters of the scene, playing techno and ambient music, although **Shiva Valley** next door has taken over in recent years.

Lilliput, a few hundred metres north of **Curlies**, www.cafelilliput.com. Lots of live music and fire-dancing performances at this beach shack – usually after the flea market on Wed and sometimes on Fri. Also has an a/c internet booth.

Paradiso, on clifftop next to **Zoori's**. Looking like a wild Fred Flintstone flight of fancy, Paradiso advertises itself as a performance art space, but it's dyed-in-the-wool techno.

Vagator *p57*

Hilltop, Little Vagator Hill, above Vagator. Although it has suffered from the 2200 curfew, Hilltop has been inventive with day parties Sun 1600-2200 and Funky Friday markets with DJs and live music.

Nine Bar, Ozran Beach. A booming mud-packed bar with huge gargoyle adornments and a manic neon man carved out of the fountain. Majestic sunset views.

Arambol *p60, map p59*

Live music and performances are the highlight of being in Arambol. **Ash**, **Surf Club**, **Coco Loco** and **Psybar** offer up both live music and DJ nights. **Arkan Bar** and **Loekie's** have open mic nights. Special mention goes to **Ash**, a stunning performance space with beautiful artwork hosting nights as diverse as mesmerizing bellydancing performances, Siberian shamanic singing or fantastic fire dancing. At dusk there's normally drumming, dancing and high spirits outside **Full Moon** on the beach to celebrate the sun going down on another day.

Morjim to Asvem *p61*

With pricey drinks and sometimes entry fees, the venues in Morjim and Aswem are mostly Russian affairs, but **Shanti** is a fun and welcoming place. Check www.sashanti.com for listings – it has a chic seafront locale and great music know-how as they also run a renowned club in Moscow and the fun boutique house bar at the Saturday Night Market. Guest DJs from Russia and Europe feature highly on the playlist, but great coups have been Talvin Singh and DJ Cheb i Sabbah, as well as great resident DJs like Phabi-D and her all-woman show Fatale Beats. Special mention also goes to **Liquid Sky** the brainchild of DJ Axailles, high on the hill above Asvem beach and with an inside dancefloor for post 2200 high jinx, this has been extremely popular since opening in

2009. Serving up minimal techno and the occasional trance beat.

Mandrem *p61*
The Prawn Factory, North Beach, Junas Waddo. Literally an old prawn factory set in the palm grove, it has been turned into a dance venue with varying success. One season it's on, the next it's off, but keep your eyes peeled for flyers.

🎭 Entertainment

Calangute *p51, map p52*
Heritage Kathakali Theatre, Hotel Sunflower, opposite the football ground, Calangute Beach Rd, T0832-258 8059. Daily in season, 1800-2000. The breathtakingly elaborate mimes of 17th-century Keralan mime dance drama take over 12 hrs to perform in the southern state. Here, however, it comes abbreviated for tourist attention spans: watch the players apply their make-up, brief background of the dance, then a snatch of a classic dance-drama.
Kerkar Art Complex, Holiday St, Calangute. Chic restaurant hosts traditional Indian dance and classical music, Tue 1830. Under new management, there is a combined dinner/ music price.

🎉 Festivals and events

Calangute *p51, map p52*
Mar Carnival is best celebrated in villages or in the main district towns but Calangute has brought the party to the tourists.
May (2nd week) The Youth Fête attracts Goa's leading musicians and dancers.

Mapusa *p55*
Mon of the 3rd week after Easter Feast of Our Lady of Miracles The *Nossa Senhora de Milagres* image is venerated by Christians as well as Hindus who join together to celebrate the feast day of the Saibin. Holy oil is carried from the church to Shanteri temple and a huge fair and a market are held.

Mandrem *p61*
Jan International Juggling Convention Gala performances, juggling workshops, firedancing, creative movement of a phenomenally high standard. Hosted in 2011 at **Galaxy** in Asvem, this is an event not to be missed – check out www.injuco.org.

🛍 Shopping

Do your homework before you buy: prices in tourist shops are massively inflated, and goods are often worth less than a 3rd of the asking price. 92.5 silver should be sold by weight; check the current value online, but be ready to pay a little more for elaborate workmanship. The bigger Kashmiri shops, particularly, are notorious both for refusing to sell by weight, instead quoting by the 'piece', and for their commission tactic whereby rickshaw and taxi drivers get Rs 100 per tourist delivered to shops plus 10% commission on anything sold. However, if you are buying jewellery be aware that prices for silver and gold have skyrocketed over the last couple of years, so maybe the shopkeeper isn't trying to take you for a ride! Gold prices have doubled in 3 years, while silver went up 40% in just 3 months early 2011.

Calangute *p51, map p52*
Mini markets like **Menezes** on Calangute Beach Rd or **Lawande** on Fort Aguada Rd for staples, plus adaptor plugs, water heating filaments, quince jam, wine, cashew *feni* in plastic bottles to take home, full range of sun lotion factors and brands, tampons, etc and money change. For silver, head for either of the Tibetan covered handicraft markets where the Tibetan community in exile gently sell silver, which you can buy by weight.
Casa Goa, Cobravado, Baga Rd, T0832-228 1048, cezarpinto@hotmail.com. Cezar Pinto's shop is quite a razzy lifestyle store: beautifully restored reclining plantation chairs next to plates brought over by the Portuguese from Macau plus modern-day dress from local

fashion designer Wendell Rodricks. Cool modern twists on old Goan shoes by local Edwin Pinto too.

PlayClan, Shop No S-3, Ida Maria Resort, next to HDFC bank, Calangute, T(0)9372-280862, www.theplayclan.com. Fantastic shop selling all manner of clothes, notebooks, lighters and pictures with great colourful cartoon designs created by a collective of animators and designers – giving a more animated view of India's gods, goddesses, gurus and the faces of India.

Candolim and Sinquerim beaches *p52*

Acron Arcade, 283 Fort Aguada Rd, Candolim, T0832-564 3671, www.acron arcade.com. A posh mini-mall with well-stocked bookstore (yoga, Ayurveda, Indian cookery, Indian flora and fauna, guidebooks, plus fiction and business books) and swish Indian lifestyle products (modestly ethnic cushions and throws and bedspreads, good stainless-steel items) and fancy clothes.

Fabindia, Sea Shell Arcade, opposite Canara Bank, Candolim. Branch of this great shop selling textiles, homewares and funky traditional Indian *kurtas* and clothes.

Literati, off main road, Calangute, parallel to Holiday St, T0832-227 7740, www.literati-goa.com. Wonderful bookshop in beautiful old house – it's like stumbling into someone's library. The best selection of books, novels, non-fiction and poetry you'll find in Goa. There are sometimes readings here, including an inaugural reading by William Dalrymple.

Rust, 409A Fort, Aguada Rd, Candolim, T0832-247 9340. Everything from wrought-iron furniture to clothes.

Sangolda, Chogm Rd, opposite Mac de Deus Chapel, Sangolda, T0832-240 9309, sangolda@sancharnet.in. Mon-Sat 1000-1930. Lifestyle gallery and café run by the owners of **Nilaya Hermitage** selling handcrafted

metalware, glass, ethnic furniture, bed and table linen, lacquerware, wooden objects.

Mapusa *p55*

Municipal Mapusa Bazaar, on south edge of the fruit and veg market. Fixed-price basic food supplies like rice, spice, lentils and cereals: useful if you're here long term.

Other India Bookstore, 1st floor, St Britto's Apartment, above Mapusa clinic, T0832-226 3306. Unconventional and excellent. Heavily eco conscious. Has a large catalogue and will post worldwide.

Union Ayurveda, 1st floor, opposite the taxi and bus stand. Great one-stop shop for all things Ayurvedic, herbal and homeopathic – phenomenal range of products to keep you travelling healthy.

Anjuna *p56, map p56*

Artjuna, House No 972, Monteiro Vaddo, T0832-321 8468, www.artjuna.com. Beautiful collection of mainly jewellery and clothes, but with a few nice bits of home decor too. Stunning collection of gold jewellery, but also cheaper tribal trinkets from Nagaland. Owners Moshe and Anastasia showcase quite a few local designers here as well as offering up their own wares. There's also art on sale and a great art fair every Feb. Recommended.

Flea Market, Wed, attracts hordes of tourists from all over Goa. By mid-morning all approach roads are blocked with taxis, so arrive early.

Natural Health Food Store, Monteirovaddo.

Orchard Stores, Monteirovaddo. Amazing selection catering for Western cravings. Olive oil, pasta, fresh cheese, frozen meats, etc. Locally made soaps and organic supplements.

Oxford Arcade, De Mellovaddo, next to **Munche's**. Good general store close to beach.

Oxford Stores, Monteirovaddo. For groceries, foreign exchange and photo processing.

Chapora Fort *p58*
Narayan, Chapora. Book stall,
local newspapers.

Arambol *p60, map p59*
Arambol Hammocks, north end of Arambol
Beach, near **Eyes of Buddha**, www.arambol.
com. The original and the best place for
hammocks and their flying chair designs
and now even baby hammocks.
Lamuella. Serving up the best of the
Western designers who make Arambol their
home, as well as imported clothes and bikinis
from Thailand and Europe. Stunning jewellery
for little magpies too.

Morjim to Asvem *p61*
As well as having a great little boutique
on-site with lovely clothes and jewellery from
Simona Bassi, **La Plage** has competition on
its hands from a cluster of neighbouring chic
beach shack boutiques including one little
black number from Jade Jagger. The local
ex-pats are laying bets on whether it will be
there again next season. But special mention
goes to **Dust** which sells beautifully designed
clothes in raw silk and hand-block prints
from JonnyJade and also a handful of
one-off pieces crafted by local Westerners –
www.jonnyjade.com.

▲ Activities and tours

Calangute *p51, map p52*
Body and soul
Holystamina Yoga Ashram, Naikavaddo,
T0832-249 7400, www.cyrilyoga.com.
4 classes daily, 0830, 1000, 1530 and 1630,
Rs 300 a class. All abilities. Inner healing yoga
meditation, juice bar, yoga camps and good
karma-promoting volunteer activities.

River cruises
Floating Palace, book through **Kennedy's
Adventure Tours and Travels**, T0832-
227 6493, T(0)9823-276520, kennedy@
goatelecom.com, opposite **Milky Way** in

Khobravaddo. Try a Kerala-style backwater
cruise by staying overnight in this 4-cabin
bamboo, straw and coir houseboat. You sail
from Mandovi in late afternoon, are fed a
high tea then a continental dinner as you
drift past the Chorao Island bird sanctuary.
International standards of safety. Much pricier
than a similar boat trip in Kerala.

Tour operators
Day Tripper, Gauravaddo, T0832-227 6726,
www.daytrippergoa.com. Offers tours all over
Goa, best deals in the region. Also runs trips
to spice plantations, or short tours out of
state, for birdwatching or empty beaches
in Karnataka. Recommended.

Baga *p52, map p53*
Boat trips and wildlife
Mikes Marine, Fortune Travels,
Sauntavaddo, by the bus stand at the top
end of Baga, T0832-227 9782. Covered boat,
dolphin trips, river cruises and birdwatching.
Rahul Alvares, all over Goa, based in Parra,
T(0)9881-961071, www.rahulalvares.com.
Fancy getting eye-to-eye with a cobra?
For an alternative day out in Goa, maybe
you want to handle or at least see a wild
snake. For the less wild at heart or snake-
aphobic, there are also amazing bird
watching trips and jungle camping
expeditions. You will be in expert hands
with Rahul. He organizes trips all over Goa.

Body and soul
Ayurvedic Natural Health Centre (**ANHC**),
Baga-Calangute Rd, Villa 2, Beira Mar
Complex, www.healthandayurveda.com;
also in Saligao. The **ANHC** is not for the
faint-hearted; the centre was originally built
for the local community that it continues to
serve and hasn't made many concessions to
Western sensibilities. Those checking into
the 2-week *panchakarma* can expect almost
every cavity to be flushed. They do offer
smaller, less daunting packages, like 2½-hr

rejuvenations (Rs 300), and have a herb garden where you can taste first-hand leaves that tingle your tongue (used to stop stuttering) or others that eliminate your sense of sweet taste.

Ayurclinic Goa, Baga Creek, T(0)9637-473366, www.ayurvedagoa.com. Under the watchful eye of fantastic Dr Rohit Borkar, you can get a whole host of treatments, massages and *panchakarma* processes here. Has another branch in Mandrem.

Diving and snorkelling
Goa Dive Center, Tito's Lane, T0832-215 7094. Goa isn't really on the diving map, chiefly because it has only 2 dive sites, both of which have what's known as variable, ie less than great, visibility. However, this outfit offers inexpensive PADI courses. Options range from the half-day Discover Scuba programme (from aged 10 years, Rs 2700) to the 4-day Open Water Diver programme, Rs 14,500. Snorkelling tours also available.

Candolim and Sinquerim beaches *p52*
Body and soul
Amrita Kerala Ayurvedic, next to Lawande supermarket, Annavaddo, T0832-312 5668, 0730-2000. Set inside an old Goan villa, this massage centre is geared up for the foreign tourist. Westerners are on hand to explain the philosophy behind Indian life science. The centre also teaches. A basic course takes 7 days. Courses in *panchakarma* last 6 months (Rs 7500). Rs 750 for 75-min massage.

Dolphin watching
John's Boats, T0832-227 7780. Promises 'guaranteed' dolphin watching, morning trips start around 0900, Rs 550 (includes meal and hotel pickup). Also crocodile-spotting river trips with lunch.

Parasailing
Occasionally offered independently on Candolim Beach, Rs 600-850 for a 5-min flight.

Fort Aguada *p53*
Taj Sports Complex, Fort Aguada Beach Resort. Excellent facilities that are open to non-residents at the **Taj Holiday Village**, and a separate access between Aguada Beach Resort and the Holiday Village. Rs 450 per day for the complex, Rs 350 for the pool. Tennis (Rs 450 per hr); squash and badminton (Rs 150 for 30 mins); mini golf (Rs 200). Yoga classes, scuba diving, sailing/water skiing/windsurfing/rod fishing Rs 450-500 per hr; parasailing/jet ski Rs 900-950 per hr.

Anjuna *p56, map p56*
Body and soul
Some excellent yoga teachers teach in Goa during the season, many of whom gravitate towards Anjuna: check the noticeboards at the **German Bakery**, **The Jam Connection** and **Bean Me Up** (see page 71). You'll also stumble on practitioners of all sorts of alternative therapies: reiki healers, acupuncturists, chakra and even vortex cleansing can all be bought.
Brahmani Yoga, next to **Hotel Bourgainvillea**, Anjuna, www.brahmani yoga.com. Drop-in centre for all things yogic – flex your limbs Mysore style, or try *vinyasa* flow, hatha, *kundalini*, *pranayama*. There are also 1-day workshops and regular *bhajans*. They also promote beach cleaning Karma Yoga. Deservedly popular.
Healing Here And Now, The Health Center, St Michael's Vaddo, T0832-227 3487, www.healinghereandnow.com. If you want an 'ultimate cleanse', sign up for a 5-day detox: fasting, detoxifying drinks and twice-daily enemas. Also offers parasite cleansing, kidney cleanse and wheat grass therapy.
Purple Valley Yoga Retreat (see page 57). 2-week retreats with celebrities of the *ashtanga vinyasa* yoga circuit. Beautiful backdrop for downward dog.
Watsu, Assagao–Mapusa road, T(0)9326-127020, www.watsugoa.com. Utterly amazing treatment. Working one-on-one,

Sun salutations

It's one of those funny ironies that yoga, now at the zenith of its international popularity, is given a resounding thumbs down by your average metropolitan Indian, who's much more likely to pull on Lycra and go jogging or pump iron down the gym than pursue the perfect *trikonasana*. They look with curiosity at the swarms of foreign yogis yearning to pick up extreme postures from the various *guru-jis* scattered about the subcontinent. "For them, it's the equivalent of having hoards of middle-class Indians rocking up in Yorkshire to study something we see as outmoded as morris dancing," admits Phil Dane, who runs Yogamagic Canvas Ecotel.

While some Indians look askance at the vast numbers of *firangi* yogis, others are making the most of it. Yoga is a good line of work on the subcontinent. In some places, there are certainly a fair few yoga teachers to choose from. Some are put off by the commercialization by those who see *ashtanga* yoga for example as the lowliest building block towards the greater endeavour of advanced Hindu consciousness. Asana CDs, featuring cameos from students such as Sting, only serve to irk these traditionalists. Similarly, yoga teacher Lalit Kumar, who runs Himalaya Yoga Valley in Goa, was often told that he should grow his hair, ditch his Western garb and grab a white kurta – live up to the image. He said, "Why? I'm just a yoga teacher." Many don the spiritual uniform and aim for the pedestal, both the teachers and the students reinforce their spiritual ego by telling everyone just how fit/spiritual/holistic they are.

India remains, nevertheless, one of the best places to study the ancient art, and many people who have embarked on yoga courses purely for its physical benefits also end up reaping some mental and emotional rewards. Yoga done with awareness can give you a taste of the bigger picture. Just keep asking around to find the right teacher. As Viriam Kaur, who runs the Kundalini Yoga Roof Garden in Arambol, says, "Maybe even more than finding the yoga that you most resonate with, it is essential that you find a teacher that you resonate with. You want a teacher that inspires you. But you also want a teacher that pushes your limits and makes you grow into your potential. The mantra for the Kundalini Yoga teacher as decried by Yogi Bhajan, is 'to poke, provoke, confront and elevate'!"

The large alternative communities settled around Arambol and Anjuna make good starting points if you are looking for some ad hoc teaching, but if you are travelling to India specifically to practice it's worth doing your homework first. Brahmani Yoga in Anjuna offer a great range of classes and Purple Valley offer retreats (see page 57). Purple Valley particularly attracts internationally acclaimed yoga teachers, such as Sharath Jois, John Scott and Gingi Lee; for these, you need to book far in advance, both for courses and flights. Some might baulk at seeking out a Western teacher in India, but often Western teachers have a better understanding of the needs of their students.

Good books include: BKS Iyengar's *Light On Yoga*, *Light On Life*, *Light on the Yogasutras of Patanjali*, *Practice Manual* by David Swenson and *Yoga Darshan*.

Seek out different schools in the four corners of India in Pune (BKS Iyengar), Mysore (Pattabhi Jois), Neyyar Dam (Sivananda), Anandapur Sahib (Yogi Bhajan – Kundalini Yoga) and Bihar (Paramahamsa Satyananda). There is also the International Yoga Festival in Rishikesh every year in February or March.

you are in a heated pool and the practitioner takes you through a range of movements both above and below the water. Using the art of shiatsu, this is an underwater massage which takes relaxation to a whole new level. The underwater dance makes you feel that you are flying and can give you a total release – a bit like being reborn. Highly recommended.

Bungee jumping
Offered by a Mumbai-based firm with US-trained staff, at Rs 500 a go. Safety is a priority, with harnesses, carabinas and air bags employed. There are pool tables, a bar, an auditorium for slide/film shows and beach volleyball. 1000-1230 and 1730 until late.

Paragliding
Happy Hours Café, south Anjuna Beach. 1230-1400. Rs 500 (children welcome), or at the hill-top between Anjuna/Baga, or Arambol.

Arambol *p60, map p59*
Boat trips and dolphin watching
21 Coconuts Inn, 2nd restaurant on left after stepping on to the beach. Dolphin-watching trips or boats to Anjuna, Rs 150 for each.

Body and soul
You can practise every form of yoga here including *Kundalini* – a rarity in India – as well as learn massage of all styles, have your *chakras* balanced, receive Tibetan singing bowl healing, participate in *satsang*, capoeira on the beach at sunset, do firewalking and learn all styles of dance. There are an amazing group of internationally trained therapists here, along with lots of practitioners with zero qualifications, so ask around.
Balanced View, in the rice fields behind Double Dutch, www.balancedview.com. Arambol has become one of the hubs for Balanced View – guidance to living life in clarity and awareness. Has a great following – definitely worth checking out.

Himalaya Iyengar Yoga Centre, follow the many signs, T01892-221312, www.hiyoga centre.com. Established Iyengar centre in town, 5-day courses and teacher training.
Kundalini Yoga Rooftop Garden and Healing Centre, Girka Waddo, near Temple of Dance, www.organickarma.co.uk. One of the few places in India where you can study Kundalini yoga as taught by Yogi Bhajan. Beautiful space for yoga, meditation, in-depth courses, healing sessions, Ayuryogic massage and therapeutic bodywork. Massage trainings also possible. Highly recommended.
T'ai Chi Garden, near **Piya's Guest House**. Panda has been teaching T'ai Chi and chakra healing in Arambol for many years and has a great reputation. Most courses are 3 weeks.
Temple of Dance, off shortcut road towards God's Gift and Villa Pedro, Girko Waddo. Beautiful location offering dance classes from Bollywood to Gypsy, Balinese to tribal fusion belly dance, as well as fire dancing, hula hooping and *poi*. Recommended.

Bronze casting and sculpting
One-off classes and a 3-week course in bronze casting, held every Jan with Lucie from **Double Dutch** (see Eating), a woman of many talents. Ask at **Double Dutch** for details.

Jewellery making and silversmithing
Several places on Arambol high street offer jewellery making courses; one of the best is with Krishna at **Golden Hand Designs**, on the Kinara junction before Arambol main road.

Paragliding and kitesurfing.
Paragliding is synonymous with the hill between Arambol and Keri – ask for Andy at **Arambol Hammocks** on the cliff near **Eyes of Buddha** for tandem flights and the paragliding lowdown. Check boards in **Double Dutch** or **Lamuella** for kitesurfing lessons.

Tour operators

SS Travels, Main Rd Arambol, near Om Ganesh General Store. Quality service on tours, tickets and money exchange. Also for Western Union. This is the place where all the local ex-pats go. Tried and trusted.

Morjim to Asvem *p61*
Body and soul

Raso Vai, S No 162/2-A, Morjim–Aswem road (towards Mandrem from Morjim), Mardi Wada, Morjim, T(0)9850-973458 and T(0)9623-556828, www.rasovai.com. Runs training courses in their signature treatments (Ayuryogic massage and Ayurbalancing), fusion massages encompassing traditional Ayurvedic techniques and yoga stretches (10 days, US$270, 4 days US$180), as well as offering more traditional treatments such as *panchakarma*, *swedan*, *pizhichil*, *shirodhara* and *snehapanam*, from a community oriented centre with meditation. Ayurvedic doctor on site. Highly recommended.

Tour operators

Speedy, near post office, Mazalvaddo, T0832-227 3208. Open 0900-1830. Very helpful for all your onward travel arrangements; also changes money. Very helpful, comprehensive service.

Windsurfing

Boards are sometimes available for hire at the south end of the beach for Rs 100 per hr.

Mandrem *p61*
Body and soul

Ashiyana (see Sleeping). Stunning yoga *shalas* in Balinese-style complex. There is drop-in yoga, meditation and dance here as well as courses and retreats and a range of massage and healing options in their new spa.
Himalaya Yoga Valley www.yogago aindia.com. Great morning drop-in classes at pretty *shala* but the main focus here is exceptional Yoga Teacher Training with

talented team headed up by Lalit Kumar. They run regular trainings throughout the season and then head to Europe and Thailand for the summer months. If you want to take your practice to the next level, this place is inspirational. Highly recommended.

⊖ Transport

Baga *p52, map p53*
Bicycle/scooter hire The only place in Baga to hire bikes is 200 m down a small lane past the Hacienda, on the left. Rs 40 per day, a little extra to keep it overnight. Almost every guesthouse owner or hotelier can rustle up a scooter at short notice – expect to pay Rs 150-350 for 1 day, discounts for longer periods. Those recycled water bottles of lurid orange liquid displayed at the side of the road are not tizer but petrol often mixed with kerosene and therefore not good for the engine. Better to find a proper petrol station – dotted around in Baga, Vagator and Arambol. Although alas it's not a guarantee that the petrol from the stations is pure either! Petrol is Rs 55 per litre or 65/70 at the side of the road.

Mapusa *p55*
Bus To **Calangute** (every 20-30 mins), some continue on to **Aguada** and **Baga**, some go towards **Candolim**; check before boarding or change at Calangute. Non-stop minibuses to **Panjim**; buy tickets from booth at market entrance. Buses also go to **Vagator** and **Chapora** via **Anjuna** and towns near by. Buses to **Tivim** for Konkan Railway and trains to **Mumbai**, Rs 8 (allow 25 mins).

Long-distance buses line up opposite the taxi stand and offer near-identical routes and rates. To **Bengaluru (Bangalore)**: 1830, 12 hrs, Rs 250 (luxury), Rs 450 (sleeper). **Hospet** (for Hampi): 1800, 10 hrs, Rs 350 (sleeper). **Mumbai** 1600, 14 hrs, Rs 300 (luxury), Rs 500 (sleeper).

Car hire Pink Panther, T0832-226 3180.

Motorcycle hire Peter & Friends Classic Adventures, Casa Tres Amigos, Socol Vado 425, Parra, Assagao, 5 km east (off the Anjuna Rd), T0832-225 4467, www.classic-bike-india.com. To really get off the beaten track and see India in the raw, go on an enfield bike tour with Peter and Friends. Recommended for reliable bikes and tours of Southern India, Himachal and Nepal. Also has quality rooms and a lush swimming pool at his Casa.

Taxis Maximum capacity 4 people. To **Panjim**, Rs 100; **Calangute/Baga**, Rs 150; **Arambol**, Rs 300; **Chapora/Siolim**, Rs 80. Auto to **Calangute**, Rs 50. Motorcycle taxi to **Anjuna** or **Calangute**, Rs 70, but open to bargaining.

Train Tivim station, on the Konkan Railway, is convenient if you want to head straight to the **northern beaches** (Calangute, Baga, Anjuna and Vagator), avoiding Panjim and Margao. A local bus meets each train and usually runs as far as the Kadamba Bus Stand in Mapusa. From here you either continue on a local bus to the beach or share a tourist taxi (rates above). Enquiries and computerized tickets: T0832-229 8682.

To **Ernakulam** (for junction): *Mangalore Exp 12618*, 1952 (arr 1345), 18 hrs. To **Jaipur** (from Ernakulam): *Exp 12977*, 1138, Mon. To **Margao**: *Mandovi Exp 10103*, 1650, 90 mins; *Konkan Kanya Exp 10111*, 0924, 90 mins. To **Mumbai (CST)**: *Mandovi Exp 10104*, 1038, 10 hrs; *Konkan Kanya Exp 10112*, 1846, 11 hrs (via Pernem). To **Mumbai Kurla (Tilak)** (from Trivandrum): *Netravati Exp 16346*, 0648, 11 hrs. To **Thiruvananthapuram (Trivandrum)**: *Netravati Exp 16345*, 2152, 19 hrs (via Margao and Canacona for Palolem beach).

Arambol *p60, map p59*
Bus There are regular buses from **Mapusa** and a frequent service from **Chopdem**, 12 km along the main road (1 hr); the attractive coastal detour via **Morjim** being slightly longer. It's a 2-hr walk north through Morjim and Mandrem by the coast. **SS Travels** and **Tara**, in the village, exchange cash and TCs, good for train tickets (Rs 100 service charge); also sells bus tickets.

Keri and Tiracol Fort *p60*
Bus Regular buses from **Mapusa** to Keri, then catch ferry to Tiracol Fort.

Mandrem *p61*
Bus Buses towards **Siolem** pass along the main road at about 0930 and 1345. Direct services also to **Mapusa** and **Panjim**.

❶ Directory

Calangute *p51, map p52*
Banks Many tour operators double as money changers, but there are **State Bank of India** and **ICICI** ATM on either sides of Beach Rd. Also **Bank of Baroda**, Baga. **Internet** I way, NetXcess Cyber Café, Shop No 1, Sunshine Complex, Baga Rd, T0832-228 1516, netxcess@mail.com. Broadband internet chain I way's branch is faster than most. **Nikki's Internet Café**, Calangute Tourist Resort Annexe, T0832-228 1950, 0900-2400, Rs 40 per hr, 8 terminals, café, forex, pool table. Useful during frequent power cuts. **Police** T0832-227 8284. **Telephone** Look for the yellow STD ISD signs.

Candolim and Sinquerim beaches *p52*
Medical services Health Centre, Main Rd; Bosto Hospital, Panjim Rd.

Mapusa *p55*

Banks Bank of India, opposite Municipal Gardens, changes TCs, cash against Visa and MasterCard. Mon-Fri 1000-1400, Sat 1000-1200. **Pink Panther Agency** changes Visa and MasterCard, Mon-Fri 0900-1700, Sat 0900-1300. **State Bank of India**, exchanges cash and TCs, 15-20 mins. Foreign exchange on 1st floor, Mon-Fri 1000-1600, Sat 1000-1200. **Internet** Several across town, well signposted. Most charge Rs 90 per hr. Best at **LCC**, 3rd floor, Bhavani Apartments, daily 0700-2130, Rs 15 per 15 mins, 6 terminals. **Medical services** Ambulance: T0832-226 2372. **Asilo Hospital**, T0832-226 2211. Pharmacies: including **Bardez Bazar**; **Drogaria**, near the Swiss Chapel, open 24 hrs; **Mapusa Clinic**, T0832-226 2350. **Police** T0832-226 2231. **Post** Opposite the police station.

Anjuna *p56, map p56*

Banks Bank of Baroda, Sorranto Vaddo, Mon-Wed, Fri 0930-1330, Sat 0930-1130, accepts most TCs, Visa/MasterCard, 1% commission (minimum Rs 50); also provides Safe Custody Packets. Thomas Cook agent at **Oxford Stores**, central, quicker and more efficient. **Internet** Raju's, near Blue Tao restaurant, gives you computers on proper desks, notepads for scribbling and a good connection. Rs 40 per hr, 0900-2100. **Medical services** St Michael's Pharmacy, Main Rd, Sorranto, open 24 hrs. **Police** T0832-227 3233. **Post** Poste Restante at post office, Mon-Sat 1000-1600; efficient, parcels are also accepted without a fuss.

Chapora Fort *p58*

Internet Sonya Travels, near Holy Cross. Offers foreign exchange, money transfers, ticketing and internet.

Arambol *p60, map p59*

Banks Nearest ATM is in Mandrem. **Medical services** Pharmacy on the main road opposite post office. **Health centre**, T0832-229 1249. **Police** T0832-229 7614. **Post** The small village post office is at the T-junction, 1500 m from the beach.

Mandrem *p61*

Banks Canara Bank, on the main road accepts TCs. **Medical services** Hospital, T0832-223 0081.

South Goa

The prosperous south is poster-paint green: lush coconut thickets that stretch along the coastline blend with broad swathes of iridescent paddy, broken by the piercingly bright white spears of splendid church steeples. Beneath the coastal coconut fronds sit the pretty villages of fishermen and agriculturalists: Salcete taluka is where the Portuguese were most deeply entrenched, and in the district's interior lie the beautiful fossilized remnants of centuries-old mansion estates built by the Goan colonial elite. Sprawling drawing rooms and ballrooms are stuffed with chandeliers and antiques and paved with splendid marble, every inch the fairytale doll's house.

Margao and coastal Salcete → *For listings, see pages 94-106.*

A wide belt of golden sand runs the length Salcete's coast in one glorious long lazy sweep, hemmed on the landward side by a ribbon of low-key beach shacks; tucked inland lie Goa's most imposing and deluxe hotels. The thrumming nightlife of North Goa is generally absent here, but some beaches, Cavelossim in particular, have been on the receiving end of a building boom kept afloat by Russian package tourists, while Colva has gone all out and built itself a line of Baywatch-style lifeguard shacks – buxom blonde lifesavers not included. Inland, in various states of decline, lie the stately mansions of Goa's landowning classes: worn-out cases of homes once fit for princes.

Ins and outs

Getting there and around The Konkan Railway connects Margao directly with Mumbai, Mangalore and Kerala. Madgaon/Margao station is 1.5 km southeast of the bus stands, municipal gardens and market area (where you'll find most of the hotels and restaurants). Rickshaws charge Rs 15 to transfer or walk the 800 m along the railway line. Interstate buses and those running between here and North Goa use the New Kadamba (State) Bus Stand 2 km north of town. City buses take you to the town bus stands for destinations south of Margao. Colva and Benaulim buses leave from the local bus stand east of the gardens. There are plenty of auto-rickshaws and eight-seater taxis for hire. ▶▶ *See Transport, page 103.*

Tourist information Goa Tourism Development Corporation (GTDC) ① *Margao Residency, south of the plaza, T0832-271 5204.* Also has a counter at the railway station, T0832-270 2298.

Margao (Madgaon)

Margao is a fetching, bustling market town which, as the capital of the state's historically richest and most fertile *taluka*, Salcete, is a shop window for fans of grand old Portuguese domestic architecture and churches. Sadly, in their haste to get to the nearby beaches, few tourists take the time to explore this charming, busy provincial town.

The impressive baroque **Church of the Holy Spirit** with its classic Goan façade dominates the Old Market square, the Largo de Igreja. Originally built in 1564, it was sacked by Muslims in 1589 and rebuilt in 1675. A remarkable pulpit on the north wall has carvings of the Apostles. There are also some glass cabinets in the north aisle containing statues of St Anthony and of the Blessed Joseph Vaz. Vaz was a homegrown Catholic missionary who smuggled himself to Sri Lanka dressed as a porter when the Dutch occupation challenged the island's faith. The church's feast day is in June.

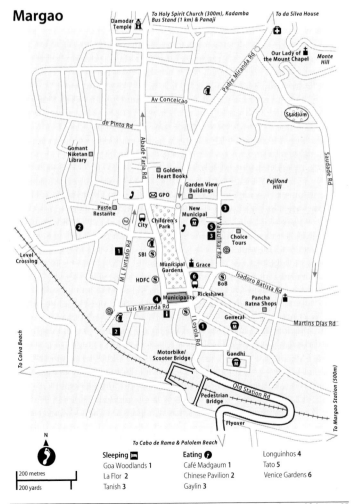

Margao

To Holy Spirit Church (300m), Kadamba Bus Stand (1 km) & Panaji
To da Silva House
Damodar Temple
Our Lady of the Mount Chapel
Monte Hill
Padre Miranda Rd
Av Conceicao
Stadium
de Pinto Rd
Abade Faria Rd
Gomant Niketan Library
Golden Heart Books
Garden View Buildings
Pajifond Hill
Saudade Rd
Poste Restante
GPO
New Municipal
Children's Park
City
Level Crossing
M L Furtado Rd
SBI
Municipal Gardens
Grace
HDFC
Municipality
Rickshaws
Luis Miranda Rd
Loyola Rd
Vaïaulïkar Rd
Choice Tours
Isadoro Batista Rd
BoB
Pancha Ratna Shops
General
Martins Días Rd
To Colva Beach
Motorbike/ Scooter Bridge
Gandhi
To Margao Station (500m)
Old Station Rd
Pedestrian Bridge
Flyover
To Cabo de Rama & Palolem Beach
N
200 metres
200 yards

Sleeping
Goa Woodlands 1
La Flor 2
Tanish 3

Eating
Café Madgaum 1
Chinese Pavilion 2
Gaylin 3

Longuinhos 4
Tato 5
Venice Gardens 6

The real gem of Margao is the glut of run-down 18th-century houses especially in and around Abade Faria Road, of which **da Silva House** ① *visits arranged via the GTDC*, is a splendid example. Built around 1790 when Inacio da Silva stepped up to become Secretary to the Viceroy, it has a long façade whose roof was once divided into seven separate cropped 'towers', hence its other name, 'Seven Shoulders'; only three of these have survived. The house's grandeur is also evident in its interiors, featuring lavishly carved dark rosewood furniture, gilded mirrors and fine chandeliers. Da Silva's descendants still live in a small wing of the house.

The **municipal market** (Mercado de Afonso de Albuquerque) is a labyrinthine treat of flower garlands, silks and agricultural yield.

Chandor

By the late 18th century, an educated middle-class elite had emerged in the villages of the Old Conquests. With newly established rights to property, well-to-do Goans began to invest in large homes and very fine living. West of the Zuari River, the villages of Lutolim and Chandor are two of a number that saw the distinct development of estates and houses built on this grand scale. Their houses were stuffed with tokens of their Europeanization and affluence, mixed with traditions appropriated from their native ancestry, installing personal chapels instead of *devachem kuds*, or Hindu prayer rooms.

Despite being something of a backwater today, the once-grand village of Chandor nonetheless boasts several fine Portuguese mansions. Foremost among them is the enormous **Menezes Braganza family house** ① *13 km east of Margao, both wings usually open 1000-1730 but confirm by telephone. West Wing: T0832-278 4201, 1300-1400 or early evening after 1830; East Wing: T0832-278 4227; a donation of Rs 100 at the end of the tour is greatly appreciated.* Luis de Menezes Braganza was an influential journalist and politician (1878-1938) who not only campaigned for freedom from colonial rule but also became a champion of the less privileged sections of Goan society. The late 16th-century two-storey mansion he inherited (extended in the 18th and 19th centuries), still complete with much of the family furniture and effects, shows the sheer opulence of the life enjoyed by those old Goan families who established great plantation estates. The two wings are occupied separately by members of the Braganza family who have inherited the property.

The **West Wing**, which is better maintained and has finer antiques, is owned by Aida de Menezes Braganza. The guided tour by this elderly member of the family – when she resides here – is fascinating. She has managed to restore the teak ceiling of the 250-year-old library gallery to its original state; the old *mareta* wood floor survived better since this native Goan timber can withstand water. There is much carved and inlaid antique furniture and very fine imported china and porcelain, some specially ordered, and bearing the family crest.

The faded **East Wing**, occupied by Sr Alvaro de Perreira-Braganza, partly mirrors the West Wing. It also has some excellent carved and inlaid furniture and a similar large salon with fine chandeliers. The baroque family chapel at the back now has a prized relic added to its collection, the bejewelled nail of St Francis Xavier, which had, until recently, been kept guarded away from public view.

The guide from the East Wing of the Braganza House can also show you the **Fernandes House** ① *open daily, phone ahead T0832-278 4245, suggested donation Rs 100*, if he's not

Living the dream?

The happy combination of easy living, tropical sun, cheap flights and the innumerable beautiful Portuguese-style houses – big porches, bright white lime walls, window panes of oyster shell and red tile roofs crumbling into disrepair – all across Goa has triggered many a foreigner's fantasy of getting their own tattered toehold in the state.

Renting is commonplace, and for US$300-500 a month you can snare yourself a six-bedroom place so romantically derelict you'd swoon.

For longer term, there are plenty of modern condos set around swimming pools, simplifying the whole process, but setting yourself up in your own 100-year-old house takes graft. Goan houses for rent are likely to be vacant because children, emigrant or living elsewhere in the state, are bickering about how best to divest themselves of the brick and mortar inheritance of their parents' ancestral homes.

This means they are unlikely to be in good decorative order. One missing roof tile opens these old houses to a violent monsoon beating. Mud and lime walls dissolve quickly, wood rots and takes in termites, and shortly the wildlife (animal and vegetable) starts moving in. Initial set up costs as most places are unfurnished could easily set you back US$2000.

Agents are springing up to act as intermediaries in what is still a largely amateurish and deregulated industry, but you will pay pretty high charges to avoid the headache of having to handle things yourself. The best representative is probably the slick **Homes & Estates**, head office: Parra-Tinto, Bardez, T0832-247 2338, www.homesgoa.com, which also publishes a quarterly magazine.

Making a longer-term commitment to the Goan property market used to be a breeze, but beware. In 2006, the state government launched a retrospective investigation into some 445 property deals brokered for foreign nationals, on the basis that many foreigners had taken advantage of Goa's decidedly lax enforcement of India's Foreign Exchange Management Act, which dictates that foreigners must be resident in the country for six months before purchases are legal.

Nor are Goan des reses quite the steal they once were: new-build 2-bed condos can cost as little as US$34,000 but rise to US$400,000.

One thing's for sure: if you are intent on joining the 5000 foreigners with homes in Goa, 3000 of them Brits, it's more important than ever to seek professional legal advice.

too busy. It's another example of a once-fine mansion just to the southeast of the village, on the Quepem road. This too has an impressive grand salon occupying the front of the house and a hidden inner courtyard. Recent excavations have unearthed an underground hiding place for when Christian families were under attack from Hindu raiders.

Back in Chandor village itself, the **Church of Our Lady of Bethlehem**, built in 1645, replaced the principal **Sapta Matrika** (Seven Mothers) **temple**, which was demolished in the previous century.

Chandor is closest to Margao but can also easily be visited from Panjim or the beaches in central Goa. It would be an arduous day trip from the northern beaches. Buses from Margao Kadamba Bus Stand (45 minutes) take you within walking distance of the sights but it is worth considering a taxi. Madgaon Railway Station, with connections to Mumbai and the Konkan coastal route as well as direct trains to Hospet, is close by.

Colva (Colwa)

Although it's just 6 km from the city and is the tourist hub of the southern beaches, sleepy Colva is a far cry from its overgrown northern equivalent Calangute. The village itself is a bit scruffy, but the beach ticks all the right boxes: powdery white sand, gently swaying palms, shallow crystalline waters and lines of local fishermen drawing their nets in hand over fist, dumping pounds of mackerel which are left to dry out in glistening silver heaps.

Margao's parasol-twirling elite, in their search for *mudanca* or a change of air, were the first to succumb to Colva's charms. They would commandeer the homes of local fisher-folk, who had decamped to their shacks for months leading up to the monsoon. The shacks have now traded up for gaudy pink and turquoise guesthouses and the odd chi-chi resort, but Colva's holiday scene remains a mostly domestic affair, beloved by Indian fun-seekers who'll willingly shell out the cash to go parasailing for 90 seconds.

Out on the eastern edge of town, the large **Church of Our Lady of Mercy** (Nossa Senhora das Merces), dating from 1630 and rebuilt in the 18th century, has a relatively simple façade and a single tower on the south side that is so short as to be scarcely noticeable, and the strong horizontal lines normally given to Goan churches by three of four full storeys is broken by a narrow band of shallow semi-circular arches above the second floor. But the church is much less famous for its architecture than for the huge fair it hosts, thanks to its association with the miraculous **Menino Jesus**. Jesuit Father Bento Ferreira found the original image in the river Sena, Mozambique, en route to Goa, and brought it to Colva where he took up his position as rector in 1648. The image's miraculous healing powers secured it special veneration.

The **Fama of Menino Jesus festival** (Monday of 12-18 October) sees thousands of frantic devotees flock to kiss the statue in hope of a miracle. Near the church, specially blessed lengths of string are sold, as well as replicas of limbs, offered to the image in thanks for cures.

Betalbatim to Velsao

A short walk from Colva, **Betalbatim** is named after the main Hindu temple to Betall that stood here before the deity was moved to Queula in Ponda for safety. This is a pleasant stretch with a mix of coconut palms and casuarinas on the low dunes. At low tide, when the firm sand is exposed, you can cycle for miles along the beach in either direction.

The broad, flat open beaches to the north – **Velsao**, **Arossim**, **Utorda** and **Majorda** – are the emptiest: the odd fishing village or deluxe resort shelters under coconut thicket canopy.

Bogmalo is a small, palm-fringed and attractive beach that's exceptionally handy for the airport (only 4 km, and a 10-minute drive away). **Hollant Beach**, 2 km further on, is a small rocky cove that is fringed with coconut palms. From Bogmalo village you can get to **Santra Beach**, where fishermen will ferry you to two small islands for about Rs 350 per boat.

The quiet back lanes snaking between these drowsy villages make perfect bicycle terrain and Velsao boasts some particularly grand examples of old mansions.

Verna

The church at Verna (the 'place of fresh air'), inland from the northern Salcete beaches on the NH17, was initially built on the site of the Mahalsa Temple, which had housed the deity now in Mardol (see page 109) and featured exquisite carvings, but was destroyed and marked by the cross to prevent it being re-used for Hindu worship. As a sanctuary for widows who did not commit *sati*, it was dubbed the Temple of Nuns.

Verna was also picked to house the fifth century BC, 2.5-m-high **Mother Goddess figure** from Curdi in Sanguem, which was under threat of being submerged by the Selaulim Dam project in 1988. Two megalithic sites were found in the area. It is surrounded by seven healing springs. Just north towards Cortalim are the popular medicinal **Kersarval springs**.

Benaulim to Mobor

At Colva Beach's southern end lies tranquil **Benaulim**, which, according to the myth of Parasurama, is 'where the arrow fell' to make Goa. It is now a relaxed village set under palms, where business centres around toddy tapping and fishing. The hub of village activity is Maria Hall crossing, just over 1 km from the beach.

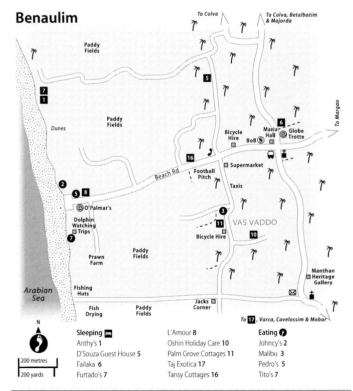

Benaulim

To Colva
To Colva, Betalbatim & Majorda
To Margao

Paddy Fields
Dunes
Paddy Fields
Bicycle Hire
Maria Hall
Globe Trotte
BoB
Beach Rd
Football Pitch
Supermarket
Taxis
O'Palmar's
Dolphin Watching Trips
Bicycle Hire
VAS VADDO
Prawn Farm
Paddy Fields
Manthan Heritage Gallery
Arabian Sea
Fishing Huts
Fish Drying
Paddy Fields
Jacks Corner
To Varca, Cavelossim & Mobor

N
200 metres
200 yards

Sleeping
Anthy's 1
D'Souza Guest House 5
Failaka 6
Furtado's 7

L'Amour 8
Oshin Holiday Care 10
Palm Grove Cottages 11
Taj Exotica 17
Tansy Cottages 16

Eating
Johncy's 2
Malibu 3
Pedro's 5
Tito's 7

On a hill beyond the village is the diminutive **Church of St John the Baptist**, a fine piece of Goan Christian architecture rebuilt in 1596. Although the gable façade, with twin balustraded towers, is striking, the real treat is inside, in its sumptuous altar *reredos* and wonderful rococo pulpit with its depiction of the Lamb of the Apocalypse from the Book of Revelation.

The picturesque lane south from Benaulim runs through small villages and past white-painted churches. Paddy gives way to palm, and tracks empty onto small seaside settlements and deserted beaches. Benaulim beach runs into **Varca**, and then Fatrade, before the main road finally hits the shoreline amid a sprouting of resorts and restaurants at **Cavelossim**. Farthest south, **Mobor**, about 6 km from Cavelossim, lies on the narrow peninsula where the river Sal joins the sea. The Sal is a busy fishing route, but doubles as a lovely spot for boat rides.

Betul

Idyllic Betul, which overlooks Mobor from the opposite bank of the Sal in Quepem *taluka*, is an important fishing and coir village shaded by coconut palms and jackfruit, papaya and banana trees. A sand bar traps the estuary into a wide and protected lagoon and the cool breezes from the sea temper even the hottest Goan high noon. Just after the bridge, which crosses the mouth of a small river, a narrow road off to the right by the shops zigzags through the village along the south side of the Sal.

From Cavelossim the shortest route to Betul is by taking the ferry across the Sal (a signposted road leads southeast from a junction just north of Cavelossim) to Assolna; turn left off the ferry, then turn right in the village to join the main road towards Betul. From Margao, the NH17 forks right (6 km) towards Assolna at Chinchinim. After a further 6 km, there is a second turning in Cuncolim for Assolna. Buses from Margao to Betul can be very slow, but there is a fairly regular service stopping in all the settlements along the way (a couple of them continue as far as Cabo de Rama).

Cuncolim

The Jesuits razed Cuncolim's three principal Hindu temples (including the Shantadurga) and built churches and chapels in their stead.

Varca to Betul

Taj Exotica **13**

Eating 🍴
Grill Room **1**
River View **4**

Sleeping 🛏
Club Mahindra **1**
Hippo Cool **4**

Bars & clubs 🍸
Aqua at Leela Palace Hotel **7**

Hindu 'rebels' killed five Jesuits and several converts in reprisal, triggering a manhunt which saw 15 men killed by the captain of Rachol Fort's soldiers. The relics of the Christian 'martyrs of Cuncolim' now lie in the Sé Cathedral in Old Goa (see page 41). The cathedral's golden bell, Goa's largest, was cast here in 1652.

Cabo de Rama, Palolem and the far south → *For listings, see pages 96-106.*

Palolem is the closest Goa gets to a picture-postcard perfect bay: a beautiful arc of palm-fringed golden sand that's topped and tailed with rocky outcrops. Under the canopy of the dense coconut forests lie restaurants, coco-huts and countless hammocks. To the north, a freshwater stream and a short swim or wade will get you to the jungle of the tiny Canacona Island.

Palolem's sheer prettiness has made it popular, prompting some travellers to drift south to the tranquil beaches of neighbouring Colomb, Patnem and Galgibaga (beautiful Rajbag is ring-fenced by a five-star). Patnem, hemmed in by crags and river at either end, doesn't have the same rash of coconut trees that made Palolem so shadily alluring and has mopped up most of the overspill. Less visited, to the north, is Agonda, a pretty fishing village strung out along a windswept casuarina-backed bay. The dramatic ruined fort at Cabo de Rama yields some of Goa's most dramatic views from its ramparts and has empty coves tucked about at its shores.

Ins and outs
Getting there The nearest major transport junction for all these beaches is Canacona, also known as Chaudi, on the NH17 between Panjim and Karwar in Karnataka. Buses from here shuttle fairly continuously down to Palolem, and less frequently to Agonda, while there's a less frequent service from the beaches direct to Margao (37 km) which take about an hour. Canacona station on the Konkan railway is only 2 km from Palolem. Canacona's main square has the bus and autorickshaw stands; rickshaws cost Rs 50-150 to any of these bays.

Getting around The area between the beaches is small and wandering between them becomes a leisure pursuit in itself. The drive to Cabo de Rama, although riddled with hairpin bends, is particularly lovely, and going under your own steam means you can hunt out tucked away beaches nearby and stop over at the fishing dock at the estuary north of Agonda. Buses run along this route between the bays roughly hourly.

Cabo de Rama (Cape Rama)
Legend has it that the hero of the Hindu epic *Ramayana* lived in this desolate spot with his wife Sita during their exile from Ayodhya, and the fort predated the arrival of the Portuguese who seized it from its Hindu rulers in 1763. Its western edge, with its sheer drop to the Arabian Sea, gives you a stunning vista onto a secluded stretch of South Goa's coastline.

The main entrance to the **fort** seems far from impregnable, but the outer ramparts are excellently preserved with several cannons still scattered along their length. The gatehouse is only 20 m or so above the sea, and is also the source of the fort's water supply. A huge tank was excavated to a depth of about 10 m, which even today contains water right through the dry season. If a local herdsman is about ask him to direct you to the two springs, one of which gives out water through two spouts at different temperatures.

Agonda

Snake through forests and bright paddy south from Cabo De Rama towards Palolem to uncover artless Agonda, a windswept village backed by mountains of forestry full of acrobatic black-faced monkeys. Local political agitators thwarted plans for a five-star hotel and so have, temporarily at least, arrested the speed of their home's development as a tourist destination. However year on year, more restaurants and coco-huts open up along the length of the beach. There's no house music, little throttling of Enfield engines and you need to be happy to make your own entertainment to stay here for any serious length of time. Less photogenic than Palolem, Agonda Bay has pine-like casuarina trees lining the beach instead of coconuts and palms. The swimming is safe and the sea wonderfully calm. The northern end of the beach, close to the school and bus stop, has a small block of shops including the brilliantly chaotic and original **Fatima stores and restaurant** (Fatima Rodrigues, not one to be a jack of all trades, has limited her menu to just spaghetti and *thali*) and **St Annes bookstore**, a video library.

Palolem

For a short spell, when the police cracked down most severely on parties up north, Palolem looked like it might act as the Anjuna overflow. Today, **Neptune's Point** has permission to hold parties once every two weeks, but so far, Palolem's villagers are resisting the move to make the beach a mini-party destination and authorities are even stumping up the cash to pay for litter pickers. The demographic here is chiefly late 20s and 30-something couples, travellers and students. The large church and high school of **St Tereza of Jesus** (1962) are on the northern edge of town.

Beaches further south

Over the rocky outcrops to the south you come to the sandy cove of **Colomb**. Wholly uncommercial, its trees are pocked with long-stayers' little picket fences and stabs at growing banana plants, their earthy homesteads cheek by jowl with fishermen's huts. The locals are currently holding firm against a controversial development planned by a Russian group, and for now the only sounds here are the rattle of coconut fronds and bird song. Although just a bay away, you could almost be on a different planet to Palolem.

At the end of the track through Colomb, a collection of huts marks the start of the fine sweep of **Patnem Beach**. The 500 villagers here have both put a limit on the number of shacks and stopped outsiders from trading, and as a result the beach has conserved much of its unhurried charm. The deep sandbanks cushion volleyball players' falls and winds whip through kite flyers' sails: but fishing boats far outnumber sun loungers. A hit with old rockers, Israelis and long-stayers, there is no nightlife, no parties and, no coincidence, a healthy relationship between villagers and tourism. Hindu temples in Patnem have music most Fridays and Saturdays, with tabla, cymbals and harmonica.

Further south, wade across a stream (possible before the monsoon) to reach the dune- and casuarina-fringed **Rajbag Beach**, its southern waters a-bob with fishing boats. Although it's virtually unvisited and has perfect swimming, the luxury five-star that opened here in 2004 has provoked a storm of protest; allegations against the hotel include the limited access to the sea, the failure to meet local employment quotas, and the rebuilding of the ancient Shree Vita Rukmayee Temple, which villagers argue was tantamount to the hotel 'swallowing our God'. The isolated **Kindlebaga Beach** is east of Rajbag, 2 km from Canacona.

Galgibaga

Nip across the Talpona River by the ferry to reach a short strip of land jutting out to sea, where well-built houses lie among lucrative casuarina plantations. Like Morjim, **Galgibaga Beach** is a favourite stopover for Olive Ridley **turtles**, which travel vast distances to lay their eggs here each November. Shacks are mushrooming, to environmentalists' concern.

Partagali and Cotigao Wildlife Sanctuary

At a left turn-off the NH17, 7 km south of Canacona, to Partagali, a massive concrete gateway marks the way to the temple. If you go a little further, you reach a 2-km-long road that leads to the Cotigao Wildlife Sanctuary. Partagali's **Shri Sausthan Gokarn Partagali Jeevotam Math** is a centre for culture and learning on the banks of the river Kushavati. The *math* (religious establishment) was set up in AD 1475 at Margao when the followers, originally Saivites, were converted and became a Vaishnav sect. During the period of Portuguese Christianization (1560-1568), the foundation was moved south to Bhatkal (in northern Karnataka). The sixth Swami returned the *math* to Partagali, and built its Rama, Lakshman, Sita and Hunuman temple. An ancient *Vatavriksha* (banyan tree) 65 m by 75 m, which represents this Vaishnav spiritual movement, is a sacred meditation site known as *Bramhasthan*. The tree and its *Ishwarlinga* (the *lingam* of the Lord, ie Siva) have drawn pilgrims for more than a millennium. The temple, which also has a typical tall Garuda pillar, celebrates its festival in March/April.

Cotigao Wildlife Sanctuary ① *60 km south of Panjim, www.goaforest.com/wildlife mgmt/body_cotigao.htm, year-round 0730-1730 (but may not be worthwhile during the monsoon), Rs 5, 2-wheelers Rs 10, cars Rs 50, camera Rs 25, video Rs 100*, lies in one of the most densely forested areas of the state. The 86-sq-km sanctuary is hilly to the south and east and has the Talpona River flowing through it. There is a nature interpretation centre with a small reference library and map of the park roads at the entrance. The vegetation is mostly moist deciduous with some semi-evergreen and evergreen forest cover. You may be very lucky and spot gazelles, panther, sloth bear, porcupine and hyena, and several reptiles, but only really expect wild boar, the odd deer and gaur and many monkeys. Bird-spotting is more rewarding; rare birds include rufous woodpecker, Malabar crested lark and white-eyed eagle. You need your own vehicle to reach the treetop watchtowers and waterholes that are signposted, 3 km and 7 km off the main metalled road on a variable rough track. There are no guides available, but the forest paths are easy to follow – just make sure you have drinking water and petrol. The chances of seeing much wildlife, apart from monkeys, are slim, since by the opening time of 0730 animal activity has already died down to its daytime minimum.

The first tower by a waterhole is known as **Machan Vhutpal**, 400 m off the road, with great views of the forest canopy. The second tower is sturdier and the best place to spend a night (permission required).

Most visitors come for a day trip, but if you are keen on walking in the forest this is a great place to spend a day or two. You can either stay near the sanctuary office or spend a night in a watchtower deep in the forest. A short way beyond the sanctuary entrance the metalled road passes through a small hamlet where there is a kiosk for the villagers living within the reserve, which sells the usual array of basic provisions. If you are planning to spend a few days in the park it is best to bring your own fresh provisions and then let the staff prepare meals. Rudimentary facilities like snake proof campsites, with canvas tents available from the forest office. You'll also need written permission to stay in the forest rest house or watchtower from the Deputy Conservator Of Forests, 3rd floor, Junta House, Panaji, as far in advance of a visit as possible.

The cheapest way to visit the park is to get a group together from Palolem. If you leave the beach just before 0700 you will be at the park gates when they open. Motorbikes are also allowed in the sanctuary.

South Goa listings

For Sleeping and Eating price codes and other relevant information, see Essentials pages 15-18.

🛏 Sleeping

Margao *p84, map p85*
With Colva and other beaches little over 15 mins away, there is not much point staying in Margao itself.
$$ Goa Woodlands, ML Furtado Rd, opposite City Bus Stand, T0832-271 5522, goawoodland@yahoo.co.in. Recently tarted up into a swish business hotel, the 35 rooms here are clean, spacious and anonymous. Restaurant, bar, good value, but mixed reports.
$ La Flor, E Carvalho St, T0832-273 1402, laflorgoa@gmail.com. 35 rooms with bath, some a/c, restaurant, clean, away from bustle of town and very pleasant for the price.
$ Tanish, Reliance Trade Centre, V V Rd, T0832-273 5656. New place with smart, good value rooms, sharing a business complex with cybercafés and mobile phone dealers. It's an OK-for-one-night kind of place. Several good restaurants nearby.

Chandor *p86*
$$$ The Big House, T0832-264 3477, www.ciarans.com. This is the stone-walled, terracotta-tiled ancestral Portuguese/ Goan home of John Coutinho, owner of **Ciaran's Camp** in Palolem (see page 97). 2 bedrooms (the master with a 4-poster, the other a twin) plus high-beamed ceilings, large sitting room, fully fitted kitchen, hot water, maid service, cable TV, DVD, phone and cooking available. Great for families, couples or groups of friends.

Colva *p88*
Most hotels are 6-8 km from Margao Railway Station. Prices rise on 1 Dec. Discounts are possible for stays of a week or more.
$$$ Soul Vacation Resort, 4th Ward, T0832-278 8144, www.soulvacation.in. Everything is uber-white here and attempting to look chic in white in Goa is very challenging as most things look a little shabby around the edges. Nice pool area and rooms with all the mod cons.
$$ C A Guest House, 470/2 4th Ward (turn right on side street north of Soul Vacation), T0832-278 0047. Cool and pleasant 2-bed apartments with balconies and basic kitchen in a huge, pastel pink house.
$ Sea Pearl, 476/4 South Ward (opposite Soul Vacation), T0832-278 0176. Not particularly well maintained, but the big high-ceilinged rooms upstairs with private bath and balcony offer the best cheap deal in town. Good seafood restaurant downstairs.
$ Tourist Nest, 2 km from the sea, T0832-278 8624, touristnest@indiatimes.com. Crumbling old Portuguese house, 12 rooms in secure new block, fan, Rs 200 with bathroom, 2 small self-contained cottages, good restaurant. Old part of house recommended for long stay (Rs 8000 per month for 2 bedrooms), spacious dining area, large lounge, antique furniture, balcony, bathroom and cooking facilities.

Betalbatim to Velsao *p88*
$$$$ Alila Diwa Goa, Adao Waddo, Majorda, T0832-274 6800, www.aliladiwagoa.com. The latest of the lush hotels to open its doors

in the Majorda area, it has already racked up a host of awards. Stunning lobby and beautiful infinity pool – beyond that the rooms are stylish and have lovely balconies. In the exclusive Diwa wing there is another swimming pool, personalized menus and bespoke packages.

$$$$-$$$ Vivenda Dos Palhacos, Costa Vaddo, Majorda, T0832-322 1119, www.vivendagoa.com. One of the most charming places you can lay your hat in Goa. Stunning renovation of old Portuguese mansion – all rooms are different; Madras has a beautiful outdoor bathroom so you can shower under the stars, The Chummery is a lovely cottage with its own veranda and you can stay in a huge luxe tent beyond the pretty swimming pool. Dinners are a fantastic communal affair although obviously you can opt out, but you never know who you might meet. Run by the hosts with the most Simon and Charlotte Hayward who come from the lineage of Haywards 5000 and their bar is dedicated to the tipple. Whole-heartedly recommended.

$ Baptista, Beach Rd, Thonvaddo, Betalbatim, T0832-288 0048. 2 simple rooms with fan, 2 self-catering flats with gas stove, use of fridge and utensils (Rs 350), good for long stays – discounts, short walk from beach. Friendly family and friendly dog once he gets to know you.

$ Manuelina Tourist House, Thonvaddo, behind **Ray's**, T0832-880 1154. 5 spacious, clean rooms with bath, TV lounge, some food available, pleasant, secure, quiet with a lovely communal veranda next to the banyan tree.

Benaulim to Mobor *p89, maps p89 and p90*
Budget hotels and rooms in private houses can be found along Benaulim Beach Rd, in the coconut groves on either side, and along the beach south of **Johncy's**, but the rock bottom deals are drying up fast. Even simple beach guesthouses don't mind charging Rs 1000 a night for a room with bath.

$$$$ Taj Exotica, Calvaddo, towards Varca, T0832-658 3333, exoticabc.goa@tajhotels.com. 23 ha of greenery and views of virgin beaches from each of its 138 luxurious rooms. Good restaurants, including Mediterranean, coffee shop, nightclub, excellent pool, golf course, floodlit tennis, kids' activities, jacuzzi, watersports, gym, jogging track, library and bike hire. Spa offers treatments like Balinese massage, acupuncture and aromatherapy.

$$ Palm Grove Cottages, Vas Vaddo, Benaulim, T0832-277 0059, www.palmgrove goa.com. 20 clean spacious but not stylish rooms. The newer blocks at rear with showers and balconies are better. Pleasant palm-shaded garden, good food, Ayurvedic treatments. Not on the beach but plenty of places to hire a bicycle just outside. Welcoming. Recommended.

$$-$ L'Amour, end of Beach Rd, Benaulim, T0832-277 0404, www.lamourbeachresort. com. Close to the sea, 20 cottage-style rooms amid pleasant gardens, in a well-established hotel run by same team as **Johncy's** beach shack. Good terrace restaurant, handy for exchange and booking rail and bus tickets.

$$-$ Furtado's, north of Benaulim, Sernabatim Beach, T0832-277 0396. Tired-looking cottages that are better inside than out; only the cheaper, nicer non-a/c versions are worth staying in.

$ Anthy's, Sernabatim Beach (2-min walk south of **Furtado's**), T(0)9922-854566, www.goaguesthomes.com. A tiny collection of simple white cottages with bed, bathroom, mosquito net and not much more, set behind a popular beach café. Simple but nicely done and on a pleasant bit of beach.

$ Failaka, Adsulim Nagar, near Maria Hall crossing, Benaulim, T0832-277 1270, hotelfailaka@hotmail.com. 16 spotless, comfortable rooms, 4 with TV, quieter at rear, excellent restaurant, friendly family set-up.

$ Heaven, north of Benaulim, Sernabatim Beach, T0832-324 6325, www.heavengoa.in. Absolutely stunning views of palm trees and green foliage, but it's 500 m from the beach. Great value rooms and deservedly popular – book ahead. Also ayurvedic massage available on-site. Recommended.

$ L'Amour, end of Beach Rd, Benaulim, T0832-277 0404, www.lamourbeach resort.com. Close to the sea, 20 cottage-style rooms amid pleasant gardens, in a well-established hotel run by same team as **Johncy's** beach shack. Good terrace restaurant, handy for exchange and booking rail and bus tickets.

$ Oshin Holiday Care, House no 126, Vas Vaddo, Benaulim, T0832-277 0069, www.oshin-guesthouse.com. You'll need a bicycle to get to the beach but the peaceful location overlooking egret and buffalo ponds is well worth it. 14 good large rooms with bath on 3 floors (room 11 best), breakfast, dinner on request, friendly manager, superb well-kept grounds. Recommended.

$ Tansy Cottages, Beach Rd, Benaulim, T0832-277 0574, tansytouristcottages@ yahoo.co.in. The simple, boxy rooms with balconies in this pair of lime-and-lilac blocks offer decent value if you can cope with oil-stained sheets and a faint odour of must. Good restaurant (super breakfast), internet, friendly.

Agonda *p92*

$$$-$$ H2O, towards south end of the beach, T(0)9423-836994, www.h2oagonda.com. Black is the new color for chic boho beachhuts in south Goa. H20 is the new kid on the block, offering up a smarter alternative, but feels a little out of place here in Goa. Great sun-loungers for sundowners, a spa on site and the food hits the spot too.

$$$-$ Shanti Village, towards south end of the beach, T(0)9823-962154, www.shantiagonda.com. With lovely views and chic huts (again in the colour of the season – black), Shanti is giving **H2O** a run for its money – being smaller than its watery neighbour, it has a more intimate

vibe. Also at another location towards the north end of the beach near **Simrose**, they have some cheaper huts, although still very nice with tribal masks and textiles to decorate.

$$ Blue Lagoon Resort, 4 km north of Agonda at Khola beach, T0832-264 7842, www.bluelagoongoa.com. Rajasthani tents set up on this secluded beach north of Agonda – blissful. There are also lovely huts, a restaurant and amazing views.

$$-$ Common Home, south end of the beach, T0832-264 7890. Innovatively designed a/c rooms with Rajasthani wooden doors, and beach huts with sleek slate bathrooms and cow dung walls – all with interesting furniture and draped fabrics.

$$-$ Monsoon, north end of the beach, T(0)9823-198025, monsoongoa@hotmail.com. Assortment of rice grass huts and some sweet rooms at the back. Looking a little shabby round the edges.

$$-$ Simrose, towards north end of the beach, T(0)9420-162474, www.simrose-goa. com. Stylish beach shacks and nice rooms at the back dotted around pretty restaurant. Restaurant has plenty of little nooks for romantic suppers or shady spots for daytime lounging. Good value – recommended.

$ Dersy Beach Resort, south end of the beach, T0832-264 7503. 50-year-old family house developed to fit 12 clean rooms with bathrooms. Over the road on the beach are 12 basic bamboo huts with spotless shared wash block. Good value generally, but in high season the huts are not worth the price.

$ Nana's Nook, extreme south end of the the beach, T(0)9421-244672. Simple beach huts dotted around a central café with shared bath. The best huts at the front offer ideal views. Recommended.

$ Sun Set, up the cliff, south end of the beach, T0832-264 7381. Simple cottages on the cliff with great views, most with shared facilities, some with attached bathrooms and kitchen. The restaurant perched high on the rocks has prime views of Agonda.

$ White Sand, north end of the beach, T0832-264 7831, whitesandbb@yahoo.co.in. Bungalows and 2-tier huts dotted around great circular restaurant, also nice spacious rooms in converted family house at back. 2-tier rooms are blessed with great views. Recommended.

Palolem p92

Palolem's popularity has soared inordinately and in high season prices go off the scale. Off season, bargain hard and ask around for rooms inside family houses. There is a wide range of accommodation.

$$$-$$ Art Resort, close to **Bhakti Kutir**, T(0)9665-982344, www.art-resort-goa.com. Colourful seafront cottages with interesting interior design from Riki Hinteregger using khadi natural cotton.

$$$-$$ Ciaran's Camp, beach, T0832-264 3477, www.ciarans10.com. Primo glass-fronted wooden huts are spaced wide apart in palm-covered landscaped gardens; many have their own roof terrace with loungers. A library, lovely shop, table tennis and great restaurant plus promises of live jazz all make it the leader in Palolem cool.

$$$-$$ Village Guesthouse, beach, off the main road, T0832-264 5767, www.villageguesthousegoa.com. Stylish renovation of an old house, which, although only 5 mins' walk from beach feels a million miles away. Beautiful rooms with a/c, TV and chic decor and quite possibly the most luxe bathrooms in Goa. Great views across rice fields from the communal veranda, and a courtyard garden in the back.

$$ Bhakti Kutir, cliffside, south end of the beach, T0832-264 3469, www.bhaktikutir.com. This original eco-friendly abode perched on the hilltop above Palolem beach has a relaxed charm. 2-tier huts with antique furniture, compost toilets and bucket baths. There is a popular super-healthy restaurant on-site offering up a selection of every grain you can think of. Renowned yoga teacher Swami Yogananda is based here and has a dedicated following.

$$-$ Cozy Nook, at northern end, T0832-264 3550. Plastered bamboo huts, fans, nets, shared toilets, in a good location between the sea and river, Ayurvedic centre, art and crafts, friendly. Very popular. Getting a bit pricey. Goa Sailing is based here.

$$-$ Dreamcatcher, riverbank, North Palolem, T0832-647 0344, www.dream catcher.in. 39 colourful plywood cottages in the coconut grove running along the pretty estuary. Cottages are quite close together. Yoga, reiki courses and ayurvedic massage centre on site.

$$-$ Ordo Sounsar extreme north end of the beach, over a small bridge, T(0)9822-488769, www.ordosansour.com. Simple beach huts nestling north of the estuary away from the business and busy-ness of Palolem Beach. Exceptional location, amazing restaurant serving up traditional Goan tastes. Highly recommended.

$ Chattai, set back from the beach, behind Bhakti Kutir and Neptune's Point, T(0)9822-481360, www.chattai.com. Fantastic coco huts, most with loungey roof terraces. Lovely chilled atmosphere.

$ Fernandes, next to **Banyan Tree**, T0832-264 3743. 2 branches of this family-run guesthouse and restaurant on the beach. Lovely wooden cottages with attached bathrooms, good value.

$ Green Inn, on the Agonda road, near Spiral Ark, T(0)7588-444937, www.palolemgreen inn.com. Exceptional location, this 2-storey guesthouse juts out into the vibrant green rice fields offering up almost a 360-degree view of nature. Nice clean rooms with flatscreen TVs and modern bathrooms, alas no individual balconies, but amazing views from rooftop restaurant.

$ Om Ganesha, next to **Dream Catcher**, T(0)9923-171298. Clean, basic rooms with bathrooms, set behind the beach. Secure.

$ Papillon south end of beach, T(0)9890-507490, www.papillonpalolem.com. Good-value chic beach huts with laid-back vibe, a cut above the rest.

Beaches further south *p92*
Patnem

The following places are all in Patnem. Demand and room rates rocket over Christmas and New Year.

$$$-$$ The Hill, the hill above Colomb beach, T(0)9823-257709, free2b_bfree2b@yahoo.com. Tucked away on a jungle hill with great views of all 4 of the local beaches Patnem, Rajbag, Palolem and Colomb, you will find large luxury tents with en suite bathrooms. You get a great sense of privacy here as you are surrounded by jungle and yet are only a stone's throw away from the beaches, restaurants and nightlife. There's a deli-style restaurant too with spectacular sunset views, showcasing a range of locally produced foods, including amazing cheeses (price includes breakfast). There is also a workshop space for yoga, dance and chi kung. Highly recommended.

$$ April 20, next to **Home**, T(0)9960-916989, vickygoan@gmail.com. Smart 1- and 2-tiered beach bungalows with nice balconies and great views, formerly called **Goyam & Goyam**.

$$ Bodhi Eco Resort, north end Patnem, T(0)9545-337387, www.oasisecoresort.com. Uniquely designed white canvas rooms – one is even 2-storey, all en suite. Laid-back vibe with a nod to the environment. Beautiful bamboo restaurant on stilts hovers above the beach.

$$ Hidden Gourmet, Colomb, T(0)9923-686185, www.gourmetpatnem.com. As the name suggests this place is off the beaten track, or at least through the village and tucked away on the promontory overlooking Patnem beach. Beautifully decorated stone rooms all with a stunning ocean view and 2 mango wood and bamboo huts with stylish open-roofed bathrooms. Recommended.

$$-$ Home Guesthouse, Patnem, T0832-264 3916, homeispatnem@yahoo.com. Vibey rooms with nice decor make these a cut above the rest – deservedly popular. Quality linen and fairy lights make for good ambience, although opt for a room set back from the kitchen and very popular restaurant.

$$-$ Papayas, Patnem, T(0)9923-079447, www.papayasgoa.com. Eco-friendly huts running on solar power with beautifully kept gardens. Chilled atmosphere set behind small beachfront restaurant.

$ Bonkers, south end Patnem beach, T(0)9822-664026, rocking.bonkers@gmail.com. Floppy fringed palm huts borrowing their design from neighbours **Lotus Yoga**, laid back vibe at the quieter end of the beach.

$ Namaste, Patnem, T(0)9850-477189, namaste_patnem@yahoo.in. Variety of wooden huts and bamboo bungalows – good value. Nice vibe and lively restaurant.

$ Secret Garden, Patnem Rd, T(0)9850-925668, smartsheikh@redirrmail.com. Set behind Patnem beach on the little strip leading to the main road, these rooms are tucked away in a very pretty garden.

$ Solitude Dream Woods, Patnem, T0832-327 7081, solitudedreamwoods@yahoo.com. Basic plywood structures, but good value and all with attached bathroom. There is a yoga space here and swinging chairs dotted around.

🍴 Eating

Margao *p84, map p85*

$$ Chinese Pavilion, M Menezes Rd (400 m west of Municipal Gardens). Chinese. Smart, a/c, good choice.

$$ Gaylin, 1 V Valaulikar Rd. Chinese. Tasty hot Szechuan, comfortable a/c.

$$ Longuinhos, near the Municipality. Goan, North Indian. Open all day for meals and snacks, bar drinks and baked goodies.

$$ Tato, G-5 Apna Bazaar, Complex, V Valaulikar Rd. Superb vegetarian, a/c upstairs.

$$ Venice Gardens, near Our Lady of Grace Church, opposite Lohia Maidan, T0832-271

0505. Little garden oasis in the middle of Margao offering up the usual fare.
$ Café Madgaum, near Railway Gate. Good South Indian snacks.

Colva p88

$ Joe Con's, 4th Ward. Excellent fresh fish and Goan dishes, good value.
$ Sagar Kinara, 2 mins back from beach overlooking the main road junction. Rare pure-veg restaurant, offering good value *thalis* and biryanis on a breezy terrace.
$ Viva Goa, 200 m south of roundabout at east end of town. Local favourite, serving proper Goan food on red checked tablecloths. Recommended.

Betalbatim to Velsao p88

It's worth coming to Majorda for the food, there are a range of great restaurants.
$$$ Fusion, Majorda Beach Rd, Pacheco Vaddo, T0832-288 1694. Winning a Times Food Award in 2011, this place offers up a lot of meat. Steaks and carpaccio are their specialities, but naturally there are some fish and veg options too. And leave room for their chocolate fondant.
$$$ Martin's Corner, Betalbatim (coming from the south, look for sign on left after village), T0832-648 1518. Huge place in front of an old house, serving great seafood including lobster, tiger prawns and crab. As cricket superstar Sachin Tendulkar has bought a house here, it's become the hangout of choice for holidaying cricket stars and media types.
$$$ Miyabi, Majorda Beach Rd, T(0)9767-704244. Serving up for-real Japanese food – fresh sushi, tasty tempura and all sorts of fish dishes. Beautiful restaurant run by Japanese/Russian couple. Recommended.
$$$ Yum Yum Tom Yum, opposite Alila Diwa Goa, T(0)9049-775449. Recently moved from Palolem, offers up great Thai food under the watchful eye on one careful Thai lady owner.

$$$ Zeebop, Utorda Beach, follow signs to Kenilworth resort, www.zeebopbythesea.com. Lovely beach front restaurant offering up a delicious range of seafood, try the crab papads and great goan specialities. Recommended.
$$ Roytanzil Garden Pub, set back from the beach at the end of Majorda beach road past **Martin's Corner** (no sea views). Neat grounds, alfresco and small covered area. Seafood and Indian. One of the best restaurants on the south coast.

Benaulim to Mobor *p89, maps p89 and p90*
Beach shacks all down the coast offer Goan dishes and seafood at reasonable prices.
$$ La Afra, Tamborin, Fatrade. Excellent steaks and fresh fish, sensibly priced. Boatmen ferry holidaymakers to **River Sal**, Betul.
$$ Pedro's, by the car park above the beach, Benaulim. Good seafood and tandoori. Imaginative menu, friendly.
$$ River View, Cavelossim. Tranquil, open-air location, overlooking the river. Wide choice, international menu, good ambience despite being surrounded by ugly hotels. Cocktails Rs 100, sizzlers Rs 150-200, tiger prawns Rs 500.
$ D'Souza's (see Sleeping). Good juices, *lassis* and fast food.
$ Goan Village, lane opposite Dona Sylvia, Cavelossim. The best in the area for all cuisines.
$ Johncy's, Benaulim. Varied menu, good seafood, big portions, tandoori recommended (after 1830) but service can be erratic. Pleasant atmosphere though; backgammon, scrabble.
$ Malibu, Benaulim. Lush garden setting for spicy fish/meat kebabs.

Cabo de Rama p91

$ Pinto's Bar, near the fort entrance. Offers meals and cool drinks on a sandy shaded terrace, may also have rooms available. If there are few visitors about (most likely) ask here for a meal before exploring the fort to save time waiting later.

Agonda *p92*

Most of the places recommended for accommodation also have good food, especially H2O and Monsoon.

$$ Blue Planet, Palolem–Agonda road, 5 km before Agonda, T0832-264 7448, www.blueplanet-cafe.com. This Palolem institution has taken a risk and moved into the countryside just outside Agonda – but it's a beautiful risk to take. Great drive and lovely view from their new abode. On the menu, you will find an array of vegetarian and organic healthy treats.

$$ White Sand, north end of beach. Comfortable laid-back circular restaurant offering up great salads, lots of fresh fish and delicious desserts.

$ Greek Place, opposite H2O. This hardy perennial of the Agonda scene has moved from the crossroads, but serves up memorable souvlaki and greek treats.

$ Madhu, north end of beach, T(0)9423-813140, www.madhuhuts.com. Always packed, this beach shack serves up a great range of traditional spicy Goan food as well as a range of Indian, Chinese and continental food. Also has nice huts available.

Palolem *p92*

$$ Bhakti Kutir (see Sleeping). Excellent fresh fish dishes, homegrown organic produce and fresh juices. Name any number of obscure nutritious grains and they'll be here.

$$ Café Inn, at the beach road junction. Funky courtyard cafe serving up quality cappuccinos, a huge array of juices, tortilla wraps and unusual pancakes like strawberry and meringue.

$$ The Cheeky Chapatti, Main Rd. Tasty fusion food like Kingfish wraps and feta burgers with chilli jam, topped off with legendary lemon tart. Sun dinners are a great event.

$$ Dropadi Beach Restaurant and Bar. Routinely packed out. Lobster and lasagne and North Indian food are the specials – the ex-pat community do rave about the quality of the fish here.

$$ Ordo Sansour, over bridge at far north end of beach. Simple menu focusing on Goan food – strangely a rarity in these parts. Fantastic stuffed mackerel, calamari masala, Goan-style fishcakes, unique papaya curry, fried plantain chips – exceptional stuff. Highly recommended.

$$ Spiral Ark, on the Palolem–Agonda road, T0832-264 3870, spiralark@gmail.com. Great food in this vibey courtyard café – tasty thalis, organic salads, and great desserts – and a shop with beautiful textiles, clothes and deli.

$ Banyan Tree, near **Dreamcatcher** (see Sleeping). Sitting in the shade of a lovely banyan tree, the menu here focuses on Thai food and mostly gets it just right – good *pad thai* and green curries. Open mic night on Fri.

$ Shiva Sai, off main road. Great cheap *thalis*.

$ Tibet Bar and Restaurant, Main Rd, T(0)9822-142775. Super-fresh ingredients in these excellent Himalayan dishes. Small restaurant that's worth stepping back from the beach for.

Beaches further south *p92*

Nestled between Palolem and Patnem is Colomb Bay with a few huts, restaurants and the main venue **Neptune's Point**. Most of the places mentioned for accommodation in Patnem also serve up great food.

$$ Hidden Gourmet, Colomb, T(0)9923-686185, www.gourmetpatnem.com. Passionate about their food, the team here serves up a great range of fish and steaks, crisp salads and delicious desserts – all with a stunning view of Patnem beach.

$$ Home, Patnem. Great range of salads, pastas, and veggie specials like beetroot and vodka risotto – make sure you leave room for their legendary desserts like chocolate brownie and sharp lemon tart – with a very chilled chic beachfront vibe.

$$ Magic View, Colomb, in front of **Hidden Gourmet**, T(0)9960-917287. Remarkably popular Italian restaurant delivering fantastic pizzas served up on tree trunks, deliciously decadent pastas like gorgonzola and fish specials – choose from 2 views, one over-looking the rocks at Colomb and the other gazing over Patnem.

$ Boom Shankar, Colomb, T(0)9822-644035. The latest 'in' place for sundowners, this place also offers a great range of food and rooms to rent; all have great views over the rocks.

$ Mamoos, set back from beach, T0832-264 4261. Recently moved from downtown Palolem, Mamoos has served up excellent North Indian food at great prices for years.

♦ Bars and clubs

Colva p88
Boomerang, on the beach a few shacks north of **Pasta Hut**. Appealing sea-view drinking hole with pool table, sociable circular bar, dancefloor (music veers wildly from cool to cheesy), and daytime massages courtesy of Gupta.

Johnny Cool's, halfway up busy Beach Rd. Scruffy surroundings but popular for chilled beer and late-night drinks.

Splash, on beach, 500 m south of main car park. *The* place for music, dancing and late drinking, open all night, trendy, very busy on Sat (full after 2300 Mon-Fri in season), good cocktails, poor bar snacks. May not appeal to all, especially unaccompanied girls.

Benaulim to Mobor p89, maps p89 and p90
Aqua, Leela Palace, Mobor. A gaming room and cigar lounge which turns into a late-night disco after 2000.

Palolem p92
Cuba Beach Cafe, Palolem road, behind Syndicate Bank, T0832-264 3449. Cool, upbeat bar for a sundowner with regular sunset DJ sessions.

Hare Krishna Hare Ram, Patnem. Latest place for sunsets and dancing run by old schoolmates, local boys done good.

Laguna Vista, Colomb. Come here on Fri nights for French singer Axailles accompanied by Indian classical musicians – great vibe.

Neptune's Point Bar and Restaurant, T(0)9822-584968. Wide dancefloor nestled between the rocks for a mellow daily chill-out from 1700-2200 with a proper party on a weekly basis. This is also the venue for Silent Noise headphone parties (www.silentnoise.com) – an ingenious way to defy the 2200 curfew. Plugged in via wireless 'phones, you can dance your heart out to a choice of 2 DJs and there's no noise pollution. A giant screen plays movies on Wed nights.

✪ Festivals and events

Chandor p86
6 Jan Three Kings Festival Crowds gather on each year at Epiphany for the Three Kings Festival, which is similarly celebrated at Reis Magos, with a big fair, and at Cansaulim (Quelim) in southern Goa. The 3 villages of Chandor (Cavorim, Guirdolim and Chandor) come together to put on a grand show. Boys chosen from the villages dress up as the 3 kings and appear on horseback carrying gifts of gold, frankincense and myrrh. They process through the village before arriving at the church where a large congregation gathers.

Colva p88
12-18 Oct (Mon that falls between these dates) **Fama of Menino Jesus** when thousands of pilgrims flock to see the statue in the Church of our Lady of Mercy in the hope of witnessing a miracle.

Benaulim to Mobor p89, maps p89 and p90
24 Jun Feast of St John the Baptist (Sao Joao) in Bernaulim gives thanks for the arrival of the monsoon. Young men wearing crowns of leaves and fruits tour the area singing for gifts. They jump into wells (which are usually full) to commemorate the movement of St John in his mother's womb when she was visited by Mary, the mother of Jesus.

Palolem *p92*
Feb Rathasaptami The Shri Malikarjuna
Temple 'car' festival attracts large crowds.
Apr Shigmo, also at the Shri Malikarjuna
Temple, also very popular.

O Shopping

Margao *p84, map p85*
The Old Market was rehoused in the 'New'
(Municipal) Market in town. The **covered
market** (Mon-Sat 0800-1300, 1600-2000)
is fun to wander around. It is not at all touristy
but holidaymakers come on their shopping
trip to avoid paying inflated prices in the
beach resorts. To catch a glimpse of the early
morning arrivals at the **fish market** head
south from the Municipal Building.

Books and CDs
Golden Heart, off Abbé Faria Rd, behind
the GPO. Closed 1300-1500. Bookshop.
Nanutel Hotel. Small bookshop.
Trevor's, 5 Luis Miranda Rd. Sells CDs.

Clothes
J Vaz, Martires Dias Rd, near Hari Mandir,
T0832-272 0086. Good-quality men's tailor.
MS Caro, Caro Corner. An extensive range
including 'suiting', and will advise on tailors.

Benaulim to Mobor *p89, maps p89 and p90*
Khazana, Taj Exotica, Benaulim. A veritable
treasure chest (books, crafts, clothes) culled
from across India. Pricey.
Manthan Heritage Gallery, main road.
Quality collection of art items.

Palolem *p92*
Chim, main Palolem Beach road. Good
collection of funky Indian-inspired clothes
and *kurtas*, as well as bikinis and accessories.
Spiral Ark, on Palolem–Agonda road. Great
range of mainly organic fabrics from across
India. Also lots of beautiful wooden toys and

trinkets, delicious food stuffs from the deli
and everything from organic turmeric to
local frankincense from Karnataka.

▲ Activities and tours

Colva *p88*
Tour operators
Meeting Point, Beach Rd, opposite **William
Resort**, T0832-278 8003. Mon-Sat 0830-1900
(opens later if busy). Very efficient, reliable
flight, bus and train booking service,

Betalbatim to Velsao *p88*
Watersports
Goa Diving, Bogmalo; also at **Joet's**, and
based Chapel Bhat, Chicalim, T0832-255 5117,
goadiving@sancharnet.in. PADI certification
from Open Water to Assistant Instructor.
Splash Watersports, Bogmalo, T0832-
240 9886. Run by Derek, a famous Indian
champion windsurfer. Operates from a shack
on the beach just below **Joet's**, providing
parasailing, windsurfing, waterskiing, trips to
nearby islands; during the high season only.

Benaulim to Mobor *p89, maps p89 and p90*
Body and soul
At **Taj Exotica**, Benaulim, yoga indoors or on
the lawn. Also aromatherapy, reflexology.

Dolphin watching
The trips are scenic and chances of seeing
dolphin are high, but it gets very hot (take a
hat, water and something comfy to sit on).
Groups of dolphins here are usually seen
swimming near the surface. Most hotels
and cafés offer boat trips, including **Café
Dominick** in Benaulim (signs on the beach).
Expect to pay Rs 250-300 per person.
Betty's Place, in a road opposite the Holiday
Inn in Mobor, T0832-287 1456. Offers dolphin
viewing (0800-1000, Rs 300), birdwatching
(1600, Rs 250) and sunset cruises up the river
Sal River (1700, Rs 200). Recommended.

Agonda *p92*
Boat hire and cruises
Monsoon, **Madhu** and **Om Sai** hotels organize trips to the spice plantations and boat trips to Butterfly and Cola beaches. **Aquamer** rents kayaks.

Palolem *p92*
Boat hire and cruises
You can hire boats to spend a night under the stars on the secluded Butterfly or Honeymoon beaches, and many offer dolphin-watching and fishing trips. You can see the dolphins from dry land around Neptune's Point, or ask for rowing boats instead of motorboats if you want to reduce pollution. Mornings 0830-1230 are best. Arrange through **Palolem Beach Resort**, travel agents or a fisherman. About Rs 600 for a 1-hr trip for 4 people, Rs 1500 for 3 hrs. Take sunscreen, shirt, hat and water.
Ciaran's Camp, T0832-264 3477. Runs 2-hr mountain bike tours or charter a yacht overnight through Ciaran's bar for Rs 8000.
Goa Sailing, moored at **Cozy Nook** in Palolem, T(0)9850-458865, www.goasailing.com. With 3 catamarans for hire with Matthew Taylor at the helm, a qualified Royal Yachting Association instructor, Palolem makes for a great experience in sailing or learning the ropes.

Body and soul
Harmonic Healing Centre, Patnem, T(0)9822-512814, www.harmonicgoa.com. With an enviable location high above the north end of Patnem beach, you can perform your *asanas* while looking out to sea. You can have massage with just the sky and the cliffs as a backdrop. Drop-in yoga, Bollywood and Indian classical dance classes and a full range of alternative treatments are on offer. The owner Natalie Mathos also runs 2-week non-residential reiki courses and yoga retreats from Nov-Mar.

Lotus Yoga Retreats, south end Patnem beach, T(0)9604-290688, www.lotus-yoga-retreat.com. Offering up a range of yoga holidays and retreats with guest teachers from Europe, Lotus has an enviable location at the relaxed end of Patnem beach. Beautiful yogashala and stylish accommodation made from local materials.

Language and cooking courses
Sea Shells Guest House, on the main road. Hindi and Indian cookery classes.

Tour operators
Rainbow Travels, T0832-264 3912. Efficient flight and train bookings, exchange, Western Union money transfer, safe deposit lockers (Rs 10 per day), good internet connection.

⊖ Transport

Margao *p84, map p85*
Bus All state-run local and long-distance buses originate from the **Kadamba Bus Stand** 2 km to the north of town, T0832-271 4699. Those from the south also call at the **local bus stand** west of the municipal gardens, and buses for Colva and Benaulim can be boarded near the Kamat Hotel southeast of the gardens. From the Kadamba stand, city buses motorcycle taxis (Rs 15) can get you to central **Margao**.
Frequent services to **Benaulim**, **Colva** and non-stop to **Panjim** (1 hr, buy tickets from booth at Platform 1. Several a day to Betul, **Cabo da Rama**, **Canacona** and Palolem. Daily to **Gokarna** (1500), but trains are much quicker.
Private buses (eg **Paulo Travels**, Cardozo Building opposite bus stand, T0832-243 8531), to **Bengaluru** (**Bangalore**) (15 hrs); **Mangalore** (8-10 hrs); **Mumbai** (**Dadar/ CST**) (16 hrs), Rs 600 (sleeper); **Pune** (13 hrs).

Car hire Sai Service, T0832-241 7063. Rs 1000-2000 per day with driver.

Rickshaw Most trips in town should cost Rs 30-40; main bus stand to railway Rs 50. The prepaid rickshaw booth outside the station main entrance has high rates but probably better than bartering on the street. Motorcycle taxi drivers hang around quoting cheaper (but still overpriced) fares. Avoid tourist taxis: they can be 5 times the price.

Train Enquiries, T0832-271 2790. The new station on the broad gauge network is 1 km southwest of central Margao. The reservation office on the 1st floor, T0832-271 2940, is usually quick and efficient, with short queues. Mon-Sat 0800-1400, 1415-2000, Sun 0800-1400. Tickets for **Mumbai**, **Delhi** and **Hospet** (for **Hampi**) should be booked well ahead.

Konkan Kanya Express (night train) and Mandovi Express (day train) from **Mumbai** also stop at **Tivim** (for northern beaches; take the local bus into Mapusa and from there catch another bus or take a taxi) and **Karmali** (for Panjim and Dabolim airport) before terminating at **Margao**. Both are very slow and take nearly 12 hrs. From **Mumbai** (**CST**): Mandovi Exp 10103, 0515 (arrives 1815; 13 hrs), doesn't stop at Pernem; Konkan Kanya Exp 10111, 2250 (arrives 1045).

To **Delhi** (**Nizamuddin**): Goa Exp 12779, 1549, 35 hrs. Rajdhani Exp 12431, 1020, Wed, Fri, Sat, 26 hrs; Goa Sampark Kranti Exp 12449, 1120, Tue, Wed, 30 hrs. **Ernakulam** (**Jn**): Mangala Lakshaweep Exp 12618, 1935, 16 hrs. **Hospet** (for **Hampi**): Amaravati Express 18048, 0800, Tue, Thu, Fri, Sun, 7 hrs. **Mumbai** (**CST**): Mandovi Exp 10104, 0940, 11½ hrs (via Karmali, Tivim); Konkan Kanya Exp 10112, 1800, 12 hrs (via Karmali, Tivim, Pernem). **Mumbai** (**Lokmanya Tilak**): Netravati Exp 16346, 0555, 11 hrs (via Karmali, Tivim). **Thiruvananthapuram** (**Trivandrum**): Rajdhani Exp 12432, 1235, Mon, Wed, Thu, 18 hrs (via Mangalore, 5 hrs, and Ernakulam, 13 hrs). Netravati Exp 16345, 2250, 18 hrs (via Canacona for Palolem beach).

The broad gauge line between **Vasco da Gama** and **Londa** in Karnataka runs through Margao and Dudhsagar Falls and connects stations on the line with **Belgaum**. There are services to **Bengaluru** (**Bangalore**) Vasco Bangalore Exp 17310, 2059, Mon, Thu.

Colva p88

Air From the airport, taxis charge about Rs 500. If arriving by train at Margao, 6 km away, opt for a bus or auto-rickshaw for transfer. Buses pull in at the main crossroads and then proceed down to the beach about 1 km away. Auto-rickshaws claim to have a Rs 30 'minimum charge' around Colva itself.

Scooter hire is available on every street corner, for Rs 200-250 a day; motorbikes for Rs 300 per day, less for long-term rental, more for Enfields. Bicycles are hard to come by – ask at your hotel.

Bus/taxi Bus tours to **Anjuna**, every Wed for the Flea Market, tickets through travel agents, depart 0930, return 1730, Rs 200; to **Margao** half-hourly, take 30 mins, Rs 8 (last bus 1915, last return, 2000). Also to **Margao**, motorcycle taxi, Rs 40-50 (bargain hard); auto-rickshaw, Rs 70-100.

Betalbatim to Velsao p88

Bus Buses from Margao (12 km). The **Margao– Vasco** bus service passes through the centre of Cansaulim.

Taxi To/from **airport**, 20 mins (Rs 300); **Margao** 15 mins (Rs 200). From **Nanu Resort**, **Panjim** Rs 500, **Anjuna** Rs 750, or Rs 1000 for 8 hrs, 80 km.

Train Cansaulim station on the **Vasco– Margao** line is handy for **Velsao** and **Arossim** beaches, and Majorda station for **Utorda** and **Majorda** beaches. Auto-rickshaws meet trains.

From Cansaulim and Majorda there are 3 trains a day to **Vasco** via **Dabolim** for the airport. Westbound trains head to **Kulem** (for Dudhsagar Falls) via **Margao**.

Benaulim to Mobor *p89, maps p89 and p90*
Bus Buses from all directions arrive at Maria Hall crossing, Benaulim. Taxis and autos from the beach esplanade near Pedro's and at Maria Hall crossing. To/from **Margao**: taxis Rs 130; autos Rs 100; bus Rs 7. **Anjuna** Wed flea market bus 0930, return 1530, Rs 200; you can take it one-way, but still have to buy a return ticket.

From Margao to **Cavelossim**, the bus is slow (18 km); auto-rickshaws transfer from bus stand to resorts. From **Margao** taxis charge around Rs 300.

Bicycle/scooter hire Cycle hire from **Rocks**, outside Dona Sylvia in Cavelossim, cycles Rs 10 per hr, Rs 150 a day; scooters Rs 300 a day without petrol, Rs 500 with 7 litres of fuel. In Benaulim, bikes and scooters for hire, Rs 100 and Rs 200 per day.

Agonda *p92*
Bus/rickshaw First direct bus for **Margao** leaves between 0600-0630, last at 1000, takes about 1 hr. Alternatively, arrange a lift to the main road and flag down the next bus (last bus for Margao passes by at around 2000, but it is advisable to complete your journey before dark). Hourly buses between **Betul** and **Palolem** call at Agonda (and Cabo de Rama). Easy to visit for the day by taxi, motorbike or bicycle from Palolem Beach.

From Palolem/Chaudi Junction, auto-rickshaws charge Rs 120-150; turn off the road by the Niki bar and restaurant.

Car/scooter hire Madhu and White Sands in Agonda, hire out scooters, motorbikes and cars.

Palolem *p92*
Bus Many daily direct buses run between **Margao** and **Canacona** (40 km via

Cuncolim), Rs 20, on their way to **Karwar**. From Canacona, taxis and auto-rickshaws charge Rs 40-60 to **Palolem** beach only 2 km away. From Palolem, direct buses for Margao leave at around 0615, 0730, 0930, 1415, 1515, 1630 and take 1 hr. At other times of the day take a taxi or rickshaw to the main road, and flag down the next private bus. Frequent private services run to Palolem and Margao as well as south into **Karnataka**.

Train From **Canacona Junction** station, 2 km away from Palolem beach. The booking office opens 1 hr before trains depart. Inside the station there is a phone booth and a small chai stall. A few auto-rickshaws and taxis meet all trains. If none is available walk down the approach road and turn left under the railway bridge. At the next corner, known locally as Chaurasta, you will find an auto-rickshaw to take you to **Palolem** beach (Rs 50) or **Agonda Beach**; expect to pay double for a taxi.

To **Ernakulam Junction**, *Netravati Exp 16345*, 2325, 15 hrs, sleeper Rs 280, 3 tier a/c Rs 790, and on to **Thiruvananthapuram** (20 hrs); **Mangalore**, *Matsyagandha Exp 12619*, 0020, 6 hrs, Rs 49; **Margao**, 2 passenger trains a day, *KAM 2up*, 0630, *KAR 2up*, 1237, 45 mins, Rs 11; **Mumbai** (**Tilak**), *Netravati Exp 16346*, 0548, 13 hrs, 2nd class sleeper Rs 300, 3 tier a/c Rs 800; via Margao 45 mins; **Mumbai (Thane)**, *Matsyagandha Exp 12620*, 2010, 12 hrs; via Margao 45 mins.

Beaches further south *p92*
Bus/taxi For **Canacona**, buses run to Palolem and Margao and also to Karnataka. You can hire a bicycle for Rs 4 per hr or Rs 35 per day. Direct buses for Margao leave at around 0615, 0730, 0930, 1415, 1515, 1630 and take an hour. Alternatively, take a taxi or rickshaw to the main road and flag down the next private bus. Palolem is 3 km from **Canacona Junction train station**, which is now on the Konkan line (*Netravati Express*).

Margao *p84, map p85*
Banks ATMs on Station Rd, in market, and on both sides of the municipal gardens. **State Bank of India**, west of the Municipal Gardens. Get exchange before visiting beaches to the south where it is more difficult. International money transfer is possible through **Weizmann**, Miguel Miranda Building, near Mohidin Petrol Pump (Mon-Sat 1000-1800). There is also a branch in Colva.
Internet Cyber Inn, 105 Karnika Chambers, V Valauliker Rd, 0900-2000, Rs 30 per hr; **Cyber Link**, Shop 9, Rangavi Complex.
Medical services Ambulance T102; **Hospicio**, T0832-270 5664; **Holy Spirit Pharmacy**, 24 hrs. **Police** T0832-272 2175; emergency T100. **Post** North of children's park; **Poste Restante**, near the telegraph office, down lane west of park, Mon-Sat 0830-1030 and 1500-1700.

Benaulim *p89, map p89*
Bank Bank of Baroda, near Maria Hall, has ATM and best rates for exchange. **Bank of Baroda**, near the church in Cavelossim, Mon-Wed, Fri, Sat 0930-1330, accepts Visa, MasterCard, TCs; helpful staff. **Internet** GK **Communications**, Beach Rd. 24-hr phone, money exchange and internet with 4 terminals, book ahead when very busy, Rs 100 per hr. **Medical services** Late night pharmacy near the main crossroads.

Palolem *p92*
Banks Several exchanges along the beach approach road issue cash against credit cards, usual commission, 3-5%. **Internet** Widely available throughout the village, rates approximately Rs 60 per hr. **Post** Nearest in Canacona. **Useful contacts** Petrol **Aryadurga** HP station 1 km north of the Palolem turning, towards Margao.

Ponda and interior Sanguem

There is enough spirituality and architecture in the neighbouring districts of Ponda and Salcete to reverse even the most cynical notions of Goa as a state rich in beach but weak on culture. Once you've had your fill of basking on the sand you'll find that delving into this geographically small area will open a window on a whole new, and richly rewarding, Goa.

Just over the water lies Salcete and the villages of Goa's most sophisticated and urbane elite, steeped in the very staunchest Catholicism. Here you can see the most eloquent symbols of the graceful living enjoyed by this aristocracy in the shape of palatial private homes, the fruits of their collusion with the colonizers in faith. Ironically, one of the finest – Braganza House in Chandor – is also the ancestral home of one of the state's most vaunted freedom fighters, Luis de Menezes-Braganza.

Ponda and around → *For listings, see pages 114-115.*

Ponda, once a centre of culture, music, drama and poetry, is Goa's smallest *taluka*. It is also the richest in Goan Hindu religious architecture. A stone's throw from the Portuguese capital of Old Goa and within 5 km of the district's traffic-snarled and fume-filled town centre are some of Goa's most important temples including the Shri Shantadurga at Queula and the Nagesh Temple near Bandora. Ponda is also a pastoral haven full of spice gardens and wonderfully scenic views from low hills over sweeping rivers. The Bondla Sanctuary in the east of the *taluka*, though small and underwhelming in terms of wildlife, is a vestige of the forest-rich environment that once cloaked the entire foothills of the Western Ghats.

Ins and outs

Getting there and around Ponda town is an important transport intersection where the main road from Margao via Borlim meets the east–west National Highway, NH4A. Buses to Panjim and Bondla via Tisk run along the NH4A, which passes through the centre of town. The temples are spread out so it's best to have your own transport: take a bike or charter an auto-rickshaw or taxi; you'll find these around the bus stand. ▸▸ *See Transport, page 115.*

History

The Zuari River represented the stormy boundary between the Christianized Old Conquests and the Hindu east for two centuries. St Francis Xavier found a dissolute band of European degenerates in the first settlers when he arrived in the headquarters of Luso-India and recommended the formation of an Inquisition. Founded in 1560 to redress the failings within their own community, the Portuguese panel's remit quickly broadened as they found that their earliest Goan converts were also clinging clandestinely to their former faith. So the inquisitors set about weeding out these 'furtive Hindus', too, seeking to impose a Catholic orthodoxy and holding great show trials every few years with the public executions of infidels. Outside those dates set aside for putting people to death, intimidation was slightly more subtle: shrines were desecrated, temple tanks polluted and landowners threatened with confiscation of their holdings to encourage defection. Those unwilling to switch religion instead had to look for places to flee, carrying their idols in their hands.

When the conquistadors (or *descubridores*) took to sacking shrines and desecrating temples, building churches in their place, the keepers of the Hindu faith fled for the broad river banks and the Cumbarjua creek to its west, to build new homes for their gods.

Ponda

Ponda wasn't always the poster-boy for Goa's Hindu identity that it is today. The **Safa Mosque** (Shahouri Masjid), the largest of 26 mosques in Goa, was built by Ibrahim 'Ali' Adil Shah in 1560. It has a simple rectangular chamber on a low plinth, with a pointed pitched roof, very much in the local architectural style, but the arches are distinctly Bijapuri. Because it was built of laterite the lower tier has been quite badly eroded. On the south side is a tank with *meherab* designs for ritual cleansing. The gardens and fountains were destroyed under the Portuguese, today the mosque's backdrop is set off by low rising forest-covered hills.

Khandepar

Meanwhile, for a picture of Goa's Buddhist history, travel 4 km east from Ponda on the NH4A to Khandepar to visit Goa's best-preserved cave site. Believed to be Buddhist, it dates from the 10th or 11th century. The first three of the four laterite caves have an outer and an inner cell, possibly used as monks' living quarters. Much more refined than others discovered in Goa, they show clear evidence of schist frames for doors to the inner cells, sockets on which wooden doors would have been hung, pegs carved out of the walls for hanging clothing, and niches for storage and for placing lamps. The site is hidden on the edge of a wooded area near a tributary of the Mandovi: turn left off the main road from Ponda, look for the green and red archaeological survey sign, just before the bridge over the river. Turn right after the football pitch then walk down the track off to the right by the electric substation.

Farmagudi

On the left as you approach Farmagudi from Ponda is a **Ganesh temple** built by Goa's first chief minister, Shri D Bandodkar, back in the 1960s. It is an amalgam of ancient and modern styles. Opposite is a statue of Sivaji commemorating the Maratha leader's association with **Ponda's Fort**. The fort was built by the Adil Shahis of Bijapur and destroyed by the Portuguese in 1549. It lay in ruins for over a century before Sivaji conquered the town in 1675 and rebuilt it. The Portuguese viceroy attempted to re-take it in October 1683 but quickly withdrew, afraid to take on the Maratha King Sambhaji, who suddenly appeared with his vast army.

Velinga

Lakshmi-Narasimha Temple ① *just north of Farmagudi at Velinga, from the north take a right immediately after crossing a small river bridge*, is Goa's only temple to Vishnu's fourth avatar. The small half-man, half-lion image at this 18th-century temple was whisked away from the torches of Captain Diogo Rodrigues in 1567 Salcete. Its tower and dome over the sanctuary are markedly Islamic. Inside there are well-carved wooden pillars in the *mandapa* and elaborate silverwork on the screen and shrine.

Priol

Shri Mangesh Temple ① *Priol, northwest of Ponda on a wooded hill, on the NH4A leading to Old Goa*, is an 18th-century temple to Siva's incarnation as the benevolent Mangesh is one of the most important temples in Goa. Its Mangesh *lingam* originally belonged to an ancient temple in Kushatali (Cortalim) across the river. The complex is typical of Goan Hindu temple architecture and the surrounding estate provides a beautiful setting. Note the attractive tank on the left as you approach, which is one of the oldest parts of the site. The complex, with its *agrashalas* (pilgrims' hostel), administrative offices and other rooms set aside for religious ceremonies, is a good representative of Goan Hindu temple worship: the temple is supported by a large community who serve its various functions. February 25 is **Jatra**.

Mardol

Two kilometres on from Shri Mangesh, the early 16th-century **Mahalsa Narayani Temple** is dedicated to Mahalsa, a Goan form of Vishnu's consort Lakshmi or, according to some, the god himself in female form *Mohini* (from the story of the battle between the *devas* and *asuras*). The deity was rescued from what was once a fabulous temple in Verna at around the same time as the Mangesh Sivalinga was brought to Priol. The entrance to the temple complex is through the arch under the *nagarkhana* (drum room). There is a seven-storeyed *deepstambha* and a tall brass Garuda pillar which rests on the back of a turtle, acting as an impressive second lamp tower. The half-human half-eagle *Garuda*, Vishnu's vehicle, sits on top. A stone 'cosmic pillar' with rings, next to it, signifies the axis along which the temple is aligned. The new *mandapa* (columned assembly hall) is made of concrete, but is hidden somewhat under the red tiling, finely carved columns and a series of brightly painted carvings of the 10 *avatars*, or incarnations, of Vishnu. The unusual dome above the sanctuary is particularly elegant. A decorative arched gate at the back leads to the peace and cool of the palm-fringed temple tank. A palanquin procession with the deity marks the February **Mardol Jatra**, **Mahasivaratri** is observed in February/March and **Kojagiri Purnima** celebrated at the August/September full moon.

Bandora

A narrow winding lane dips down to this tiny hamlet and its **temple** ① *head 4 km west from Ponda towards Farmagudi on the NH4A, looking for a fork signposted to Bandora*, to Siva as Nagesh (God of Serpents). The temple's origin is put at 1413 by an inscribed tablet here, though the temple was refurbished in the 18th century. The temple tank, which is well stocked with carp, is enclosed by a white-outlined laterite block wall and surrounded by shady palms. The five-storey lamp tower near the temple has brightly coloured deities painted in niches just above the base, the main *mandapa* (assembly hall) has interesting painted woodcarvings illustrating stories from the epics *Ramayana* and *Mahabharata* below the ceiling line, as well as the *Ashtadikpalas*, the eight Directional Guardians (Indra, Agni, Yama, Nirriti, Varuna, Vayu, Kubera and Ishana). The principal deity has the usual *Nandi* and in addition there are shrines to Ganesh and Lakshmi-Narayan and subsidiary shrines with *lingams*, in the courtyard. The **Nagesh Jatra**, normally in November, is celebrated at full moon to commemorate Siva's victory.

In a valley south of the Nagesh Temple lies the **Mahalakshmi Temple**, thought to be the original form of the deity of the Shakti cult. Mahalakshmi was worshipped by the Silaharas (chieftains of the Rashtrakutas, AD 750-1030) and the early Kadamba kings. The sanctuary has an octagonal tower and dome, while the side entrances have shallow domes. The stone slab with the Marathi inscription dating from 1413 on the front of the Nagesh Temple refers to a temple to Mahalakshmi at Bandora. The *sabhamandap* has an impressive gallery of 18 wooden images of Vishnu. Mahalakshmi is special in that she wears a *lingam* in her headdress and is believed to be a peaceful, 'Satvik', form of Devi; the first temple the Portuguese allowed at Panjim is also dedicated to her.

Queula (Kavale)

Just 3 km southwest from Ponda's Central Bus Stand is one of the largest and most famous of Goa's temples; dedicated to Shantadurga (1738), the wife of Siva as the Goddess of Peace. She earns the Shanti (Sanskrit for peace) prefix here because, at the request of Brahma, she mediated in a great quarrel between her husband and Vishnu, and restored peace in the universe. In the sanctuary here she stands symbolically between the two bickering gods. The temple, which stands in a forest clearing, was built by Shahu, the grandson of the mighty Maratha ruler Sivaji, but the deity was taken from Quelossim well before then, back in the 16th century. It is neoclassical in design: the two-storey octagonal drum, topped by a dome with a lantern, is a classic example of the strong impact church architecture made on Goan temple design. The interior of polished marble is lit by several chandeliers. Steps lead up to the temple complex which has a large tank cut into the hillside and a spacious courtyard surrounded by the usual pilgrim hostels and administration offices.

Shri Sausthan Goud Padacharya Kavale Math, named after the historic seer and exponent of the Advaita system of Vedanta, was founded between Cortalim and Quelossim. This Hindu seminary was destroyed during the Inquisition in the 1560s and was temporarily transferred to Golvan and Chinar outside Goa. After 77 years, in the early 17th century, the Math regrouped here in Queula, the village where the Shantadurga deity (which had also originated in Quelossim) had been reinstalled. There is a temple to Vittala at the Math. The foundation has another Math at Sanquelim.

North of Ponda → *For listings, see pages 114-115.*

Spice Hills

There are a number of spice plantations in the foothills around northeast Ponda that have thrown open their gates to offer in-depth tours that detail medicinal and food uses of plants during a walk through these cultivated forests. These are surprisingly informative and fun. Of these, Savoi Spice Plantation is probably the most popular and the guide is excellent. Taxis from the coastal resorts cost around Rs 700 return from Candolim, but it's better value to ask a travel agent as many offer competitive rates including entrance fees.

Savoi Spice Plantation ① *6 km from Savoi, T0832-234 0272, www.savoiplantation.com, 1030-1730, tour Rs 350, 1 hr, awkward to reach by public transport, ask buses from Ponda or Banastari heading for Volvoi for the plantation*, now over 200 years old, covers 40 ha around a large irrigation tank. Half the area is wetland and the other half on a hillside, making it possible for a large variety of plants and trees to grow. The plantation was founded by Mr Shetye and is now in the hands of the fourth generation of his family, who regularly donate funds to local community projects such as the school and temple. All plants are grown according to traditional Goan methods of organic farming. The tour includes drinks and snacks on arrival, and concludes with the chance to buy packets of spices (good gifts to take home) and a tot of *feni* to 'give strength' for the return journey to your resort. You will even be offered several cheap, natural alternatives to Viagra, whether you need them or not.

Pascoal Spice Plantation ① *signposted 1.5 km off the NH4A, near Khandepar between Ponda and Tisk, T0832-234 4268, 0800-1800, tours Rs 300*, is pleasantly located by a river and grows a wide variety of spices and exotic fruit. A guided tour takes you through a beautiful and fascinating setting. Spices can be bought directly from the plantation.

Sahakari Spice Farm ① *on the Ponda–Khandepar road, Curti, T0832-231 1394*, is also open to the public. The spice tour includes an authentic banana-leaf lunch.

Tropical Spice Plantation ① *Keri, clearly signposted off the NH4A (just south of the Sri Mangesh Temple), T0832-234 0625, tours Rs 300, boats for hire Rs 100*, is a very pleasant plantation situated in a picturesque valley. Guides are well informed and staff are friendly. It specializes in medicinal uses for the spices, the majority of which seem to be good for the skin. At the end of the tour an areca nut picker will demonstrate the art of harvesting by shinning up a tall palm with his feet tied together in a circle of rope. The demonstration ends with the equally impressive art of descent, a rapid slide down the trunk like a fireman. After the tour a delicious lunch is served in the shade overlooking a lake where there are a couple of boats for hire. Visitors arriving in the early morning will find the boats an excellent opportunity for viewing the varied birdlife around the lake.

Bondla Wildlife Sanctuary

① *20 km northeast of Ponda, mid-Sep to mid-Jun, Fri-Wed 0930-1730. Rs 5, camera Rs 25, video Rs 100, 2-wheelers Rs 10, cars Rs 50. Buses from Ponda via Tisk and Usgaon stop near the sanctuary where you can get taxis and motorcycle taxis. KTC buses sometimes run weekends from Panjim. During the season the Forest Department minibus runs twice daily (except Thu) between Bondla and Tisk: from Bondla, 0815, 1745; from Tisk, 1100 (Sun 1030) and 1900. Check at the tourist office. If you are on a motorbike make sure you fill up with petrol; the nearest pumps are at Ponda and Tisk. Bondla is well signposted from the NH4A east of Ponda (5 km beyond Usgaon, a fork to the right leads to the park up a winding steep road).*

Bondla is the most popular of Goa's three sanctuaries because it is relatively easily accessible. The 8-sq-km sanctuary is situated in the foothills of the Western Ghats; sambar, wild boar, gaur (Indian bison) and monkeys live alongside a few migratory elephants that wander in from Karnataka during the summer. The mini-zoo here guarantees sightings of 'Goa's wildlife in natural surroundings', although whether the porcupine and African lion are examples of indigenous species is another matter. Thankfully, the number of animals in the zoo has decreased in recent years and those that remain seem to have adequate space compared to other zoos in India. The small **Nature Education Centre** has the facility to show wildlife videos, but is rarely used. Five-minute elephant rides are available 1100-1200 and 1600-1700. A deer safari (minimum eight people), 1600-1730, costs Rs 10. The park also has an attractive picnic area in a botanical garden setting and a 2.4-km nature trail with waterholes, lake and treetop observation tower.

Central and southern interior → *For listings, see pages 114-115.*

Sanguem, Goa's largest *taluka*, covers the state's eastern hill borderland with the South Indian state of Karnataka. The still-forested hills, populated until recently by tribal peoples practising shifting cultivation, rise to Goa's highest points. Just on the Goan side of the border with Karnataka are the Dudhsagar Falls, some of India's highest waterfalls, where the river, which ultimately flows into the Mandovi, cascades dramatically down the hillside. Both the Bhagwan Mahaveer Sanctuary and the beautiful, small Tambdi Surla Temple can be reached in a day from the coast (about two hours from Panaji).

Ins and outs
Getting there Buses running along the NH4A between Panjim, Ponda or Margao and Belgaum or Bengaluru (Bangalore) in Karnataka stop at Molem, in the north of the *taluka*. Much of the southeastern part of Sanguem remains inaccessible. Trains towards Karnataka stop at Kulem (Colem) and Dudhsagar stations. Jeeps wait at Kulem to transfer tourists to the waterfalls. If you are travelling to Tambdi Surla or the falls from north or central Goa, then the best and most direct route is the NH4A via Ponda. By going to or from the southern beaches of Salcete or Canacona you can travel through an interesting cluster of villages, only really accessible if you have your own transport, to see the sites of rock-cut caves and prehistoric cave art. ▶▶ *See Transport, page 115.*

Getting around There is no direct public transport between Molem and the sites, but the town is the start of hikes and treks in December and January.

Bhagwan Mahaveer Sanctuary
ⓘ *29 km east of Pondon on NH4A, T0832-260 0231, or contact Forest Dept in Canacona, T0832-296 5601. Open 0700-1730 except public holidays. Rs 5, 2-wheelers Rs 10, cars Rs 250. Entrance to Molem National Park, within the sanctuary, 100 m east of the Tourist Complex, is clearly signed but the 14 km of tracks in the park are not mapped. Tickets at the Nature Interpretation Centre, 100 m from the police check post in Molem.*

Goa's largest wildlife sanctuary holds 240 sq km of lush moist deciduous to evergreen forest types and a herd of gaur (*bos gaurus*, aka Indian bison). The **Molem National Park**, in the central section of the sanctuary, occupies about half the area with the **Dudhsagar Falls** located in its southeast corner; the remote **Tambdi Surla Temple** is hidden in the dense forest at the northern end of the sanctuary. Forest department jeeps are available for viewing within the sanctuary; contact the Range Forest Officer (Wildlife), Molem. Motorbikes, but not scooters, can manage the rough track outside the monsoon period. In theory it is possible to reach Devil's Canyon and Dudhsagar Falls via the road next to the Nature Interpretation Centre, although the road is very rough and it may require a guide. Make sure you have a full tank of petrol if attempting a long journey into the forest.

Sambar, barking deer, monkeys and rich birdlife are occasionally joined by elephants that wander in from neighbouring Karnataka during the summer months, but these are rarely spotted. Birds include the striking golden oriole, emerald dove, paradise flycatcher, malabar hornbill and trogon and crested serpent eagle.

Dudhsagar Falls

① The 2779 Goa Express leaves Margao daily at 1549, and reaches the falls late in the afternoon. It's a spectacular journey worth taking in its own right, as the railway tracks climb right across the cascades, but trains no longer stop at the falls themselves; to get to the pools at the bottom you can take a road from Kulem, where jeep owners offer 'safaris' through the jungle to the base of the falls. If taking the train simply for the view, it's best to travel through to Belgaum in Karnataka, from where there are good bus and train services back to Goa.

The Dudhsagar Falls on the border between Goa and Karnataka are the highest in India and measure a total drop of about 600 m. The name, meaning 'the sea of milk', is derived from the white foam that the force of the water creates as it drops in stages, forming pools along the way. They are best seen just after the monsoon, between October and December, but right up to April there is enough water to make a visit worthwhile. You need to be fit and athletic to visit the falls. It's no longer possible to visit Dudhsagar by train, but we have retained the following description in case the station re-opens in the near future.

From the train station, a rough, steep path takes you down to a viewing area which allows you a better appreciation of the falls' grandeur, and to a beautifully fresh pool which is lovely for a swim (take your costume and towel). There are further pools below but you need to be sure-footed. The final section of the journey is a scramble on foot across stream beds with boulders; it is a difficult task for anyone but the most athletic. For the really fit and adventurous the arduous climb up to the head of the falls with a guide, is well worth the effort. Allow three hours, plus some time to rest at the top.

By road, motorbikes, but not scooters, can get to the start of the trail to the falls from Molem crossroads by taking the road south towards Kulem. From there it is 17 km of rough track with at least two river crossings, so is not recommended after a long period of heavy rain. The ride through the forest is very attractive and the reward at the end spectacular, even in the dry season. A swim in the pool at the falls is particularly refreshing after a hot and dusty ride. Guides are available but the track is easy to follow even without one.

Tambdi Surla

① A taxi from Panjim takes about 2½ hrs for the 69-km journey. There is no public transport to Tambdi Surla but it is possible to hike from Molem. From the crossroads at Molem on the NH4A, the road north goes through dense forest to Tambdi Surla. 4 km from the crossroads you reach a fork. Take the right fork and after a further 3 km take a right turn at Barabhumi village (there is a sign). The temple is a further 8 km, just after Shanti Nature Resort. Make sure you have enough petrol before leaving Molem. It is also possible to reach the site along minor roads from Valpoi. The entrance to the temple is a short walk from the car park.

This Mahadeva (Siva) Temple is a beautifully preserved miniature example of early Hindu temple architecture from the Kadamba-Yadava period. Tucked into the forested foothills, the place is often deserted, although the compound is well maintained by the Archaeology Department. The temple is the only major remaining example of pre-Portuguese Hindu architecture in Goa; it may well have been saved from destruction by its very remoteness.

Ponda and interior Sanguem listings

For Sleeping and Eating price codes and other relevant information, see Essentials pages 15-18.

◉ Sleeping

Ponda *p107*
Ponda is within easy reach of any of Goa's beach resorts and Panjim.

$$-$ Menino, 100 m east of bus stand junction, 1st floor, T0832-231 4147. 20 rooms, some a/c, pleasant, comfortable, good restaurant serves generous main courses, impressive modern hotel, good value.

$ Padmavi, Gaunekar House, 100 m north of bus stand on NH4A, T0832-231 2144. Some of the 20 large clean rooms, have bath and TV.

$ President, 1 km east of bus stand, supermarket complex, T0832-231 2803. 11 rooms, basic but clean and reasonable.

Farmagudi *p108*
$$-$ Atish, just below Ganesh Temple on NH4A, T0832-233 5124, www.hotelatish.com. 40 comfortable rooms, some a/c, restaurant, large pool in open surrounds, gym, modern hotel, many pilgrim groups, friendly staff.

$ Farmagudi Residency (GTDC), attractively located though too close to NH4A, T0832-233 5125. 39 clean rooms, some a/c, dorm (Rs 150), adequate restaurant (eat at **Atish**, above).

Spice Hills *p110*
$$ Savoi Farmhouse, Savoi Plantation, T0832-234 0243, www.savoiplantations.com. An idyllic traditional Goan-style farmhouse built from mud with 2 adjoining en suite double rooms each with private veranda. Electricity and hot water; rates are for full board and include plantation tour. A night in the forest is memorable, highly recommended. Ideally, stay 2 nights exploring deep into the forested hills, good for birdwatching.

Bondla Wildlife Sanctuary *p111*
$ Eco-Cottages, reserve ahead at Deputy Conservator of Forests, Wildlife Division, 4th floor, Junta House, 18th June Rd, Panjim, T0832-222 9701 (although beds are often available to anyone turning up). 8 basic rooms with attached bath, newer ones better. Also 1 km inside park entrance (which may be better for seeing wildlife at night) are 2 dorms of 12 beds each (Rs 30).

Bhagwan Mahaveer Sanctuary *p112*
There is nowhere to stay inside the sanctuary; take provisions. GTDC accommodation is at the Tourist Complex in Molem, east along the NH4A from the Molem National Park entrance.

$ Molem Forest Resthouse. Book via the Conservator's Office, 3rd floor, Junta House, 18th June Rd, Panjim, T0832-222 4747.

$ Tourist Resort (GTDC), 300 m east of police check post, about 500 m from the temple, Molem, T0832-260 0238. 3 simple but well-maintained, clean rooms, some a/c, dorm, check-out 1200, giving time for a morning visit to Tambdi Surla, restaurant has limited menu serving north Indian food and beer.

Tambdi Surla *p113*
$$ Shanti Nature Resort, 500 m from temple, T0832-261 0012. Emphasis on rest, Ayurvedic treatment and meditation, 9 large mud huts with palm-thatched roofs, electricity and running water in natural forest setting. Restaurant, spice garden visits, birdwatching, hikes, trips to Dudhsagar, etc, arranged (2 nights, US$120). Highly recommended for location and eco-friendly approach.

🍴 Eating

Ponda *p107*
$ Amigos, 2 km east of centre on Belgaum Rd.
$ Spoon Age, Upper Bazaar, T0832-2316191.
Garden restaurant serving Goan meals for
locals, friendly new set-up. Occasional live
music at weekends.

Spice Hills *p110*
Tropical Spice Plantation offers tasty lunches.
$$ Glade Bar and Restaurant, Pascoal
Spice Plantation. 1130-1800. Good but pricey.

Bondla Wildlife Sanctuary *p111*
$ The Den Bar and Restaurant, near the
entrance. Serves chicken, vegetables or fish
with rice. A small cafeteria, inside the park
near the mini-zoo, sells snacks and cold drinks.

🏔 Activities and tours

Bhagwan Mahaveer Sanctuary *p112*
Popular hiking routes lead to **Dudhsagar**
(17 km), the sanctuary and **Atoll Gad**
(12 km), **Matkonda Hill** (10 km) and
Tambdi Surla (12 km). Contact the
Hiking Association, 6 Anand Niwas,
Swami Vivekananda Rd, Panjim.

🚍 Transport

Ponda *p107*
Bus Buses to **Panjim** and **Bondla** via Tisk
(enquiries, T0832-231 1050), but it is best to
have your own transport.

Bhagwan Mahaveer Sanctuary *p112*
If coming from the south, travel via Sanguem.
The road from Sanvordem to the NH17
passes through mining country and is
therefore badly pot-holed and has heavy
lorry traffic. From Kulem, jeeps do the rough
trip to **Dudhsagar** (Rs 300 per head, Rs 1800
per jeep). This is a very tough and tiring
journey at the best of times. From Molem,
a road to the south off the NH4A leads
through the forested hills of Sanguem
taluka to **Kulem** and **Calem** railway stations
and then south to **Sanguem**. From there,
a minor road northwest goes to **Sanvordem**
and then turns west to **Chandor**.

Bus Buses between **Panjim**, **Ponda**
or **Margao**, and **Belgaum/Bengaluru**
(**Bangalore**), stop at Molem for visiting
the Bhagwan Mahaveer Sanctuary and
Dudhsagar Falls.

Train From the southern beaches, you can
get the *Vasco-Colem Passenger* from Vasco
at 0710, or more conveniently Margao
(Madgaon) at 0800, arriving at **Kulem** (**Colem**)
at 0930. Return trains at 1640, arriving **Margao**
at 1810; leave plenty of time to enjoy the falls.
Jeep hire is available from Kulem Station.

🅾 Directory

Ponda *p107*
Banks UTI ATM accepts foreign cards.
Internet **Fun World.Com**, Viradh Building,
T0832-231 6717. **Useful contacts** Deputy
Conservator of Forests (North) T0832-231 2095.
Community Health Centre, T0832-231 2115.

Contents

Background

Geography → *Population: 1.3 million. Area: 3800 sq km.*

By Indian standards Goa is a tiny state. The coastline on which much of its fame depends is only 97 km long. The north and south are separated by the broad estuaries of the Zuari and Mandovi rivers. Joined at high tide to create an island on which Panaji stands, these short rivers emerge from the high ranges of the Western Ghats less than 50 km from the coast. In the 16th century, Alfonso de Albuquerque quickly grasped the advantages of this island site: large enough to give a secure food-producing base but with a defensible moat, and well placed with respect to the important northwestern sector of the Arabian Sea.

History

Some identify Goa in the *Mahabharata* (the Sanskrit epic) as Gomant, where Vishnu, reincarnated as Parasurama, shot an arrow from the Western Ghats into the Arabian Sea and with the help of the god of the sea reclaimed the beautiful land of Gomant.

Arab geographers knew Goa as Sindabur. Ruled by the Kadamba Dynasty from the second century AD to 1312 and by Muslim invaders from 1312 to 1367, it was then annexed by the Hindu Kingdom of Vijayanagar and later conquered by the Bahmani Dynasty of Bidar in North Karnataka, who founded Old Goa in 1440. When the Portuguese arrived, Yusuf Adil Shah, the Muslim King of Bijapur, was the ruler. At this time Goa was an important starting point for Mecca-bound pilgrims, as well as continuing to be a centre importing Arab horses.

The **Portuguese** were intent on setting up a string of coastal stations to the Far East in order to control the lucrative spice trade. Goa was the first Portuguese possession in Asia and was taken by **Alfonso de Albuquerque** in March 1510. Three months later Yusuf Adil Shah blockaded it with 60,000 men. In November Albuquerque returned with reinforcements, recaptured the city after a bloody struggle, massacred all the Muslims and appointed a Hindu as governor. Mutual hostility towards Muslims encouraged links between Goa and the Hindu kingdom of Vijayanagar. A Christian-Hindu fault-line only appeared when missionary activity in India increased. Franciscans, Dominicans and Jesuits arrived, carrying with them religious zeal and intolerance. The Inquisition was introduced in 1540 and all evidence of earlier Hindu temples and worship was eradicated from the territories of the 'Old Conquests'. Goa became the capital of the Portuguese Empire in the east. It reached its greatest splendour between 1575 and 1600, the age of 'Golden Goa', but when the Dutch began to control trade in the Indian Ocean it declined. The fall of the Vijayanagar Empire in 1565 caused the lucrative trade between Goa and the Hindu state to dry up. Between 1695 and 1775 the population of Old Goa fell from 20,000 to 1600; by the 1850s only a few priests and nuns remained.

Albuquerque's original conquest was of the island of Tiswadi, where Old Goa is situated, plus the neighbouring areas – Bardez, Ponda, Mormugao and Salcete. These formed the heart of the Portuguese territory, known today as the **Old Conquests**. The **New Conquests** cover the remaining areas and which came into Portuguese possession considerably later. By the time they were absorbed, the intolerant force of the Inquisition had passed. As a result, the New Conquests did not suffer as much cultural and spiritual devastation.

The Portuguese came under increasing pressure in 1948-1949 to cede Goa to India. The problem festered until 1961 when the Indian Army, supported by a naval blockade, marched in and brought to an end 450 years of Portuguese rule. Goa became a Union Territory together with the enclaves of Daman and Diu. On 30 May 1987 it became a full state of the Indian Union.

Culture

Religion While in the area of the Old Conquests tens of thousands of people were converted to Christianity, the Zuari River represents a great divide between Christian and predominantly Hindu Goa. Today about 70% of the state's population is Hindu, and there is also a small but significant Muslim minority.

Language Portuguese used to be much more widely spoken in Goa than English was in the rest of India, but local languages remained important. The two most significant were Marathi, the language of the politically dominant majority of the neighbouring state to the north, and Konkani, the language commonly spoken on the coastal districts further south and now the state's official language. English and Hindi are understood in parts visited by travellers.

Local cuisine The large expat community has brought regional kitchens with them to make for an amazingly cosmopolitan food scene. You can get excellent, authentic Thai spring rolls, Italian wood-baked pizza, German schnitzel, Russian borscht, California wheatgrass shots and everything in between. Local food is a treat, too, sharing much with the Portuguese palate, and building on the state's bounty in fresh fish and fruit. Unlike wider India, Christianity's heritage means beef is firmly on the menu here, too. Generally, food is hot, making full use of the local bird's-eye chillies. Common ingredients include rice, coconut and cashew nuts. Spicy pork or beef *vindalho* marinated in garlic, vinegar and chillies is very popular, quite unlike the vindaloo you'll taste elsewhere. *Chourisso* is Goan sausage of pork pieces stuffed in tripe, boiled or fried with onions and chillies, eaten in bread. *Sorpotel*, a fiery dish of pickled pig's liver and heart seasoned with vinegar and tamarind, is the most famous of Goan meat dishes. *Xacutti* is a hot chicken or meat dish made with coconut, pepper and star anise. For *chicken cafrial,* the meat is marinated in pepper and garlic and braised over a fire.

'Fish curry rice', is the Goan staple (the equivalent of England's fish'n'chips or ham and eggs). Most beach shacks offer a choice of fish depending on the day's catch. *Apa de camarao* is a spicy prawn pie and *reichado* is usually a whole fish, cut in half, and served with a hot *masala* sauce. *Bangra* is mackerel and *pomfret* a flat fish; fish *balchao* is a preparation of red masala and onions used as a sauce for prawns or kingfish. *Seet corri* (fish curry) uses coconut. Spicy pickles and chutneys add to the rich variety of flavours.

Goan bread is good. *Undo* is a hard-crust round bread. *Kankonn*, hard and crispy and shaped like a bangle, may be dunked in tea. *Pole* is like chapatti, often stuffed with vegetables. The Goan version of the South Indian *iddli* is the *sanaan*. The favourite dessert is *bebinca*, a layered coconut and jaggery treat of egg yolks and nutmeg. Other sweets include *dodol*, a mix of jaggery and coconut with rice flour and nuts, *doce*, which looks like the North Indian *barfi*, *mangada*, a mango jam, and *bolinhas*, small round semolina cakes.

There are also delicious fruits: *alfonso* mangos in season, the rich jackfruit, papaya, watermelons and cashew nuts.

Drinks in Goa remain relatively cheap compared to elsewhere in India thanks to the state's low taxes. The fermented juice of cashew apples is distilled for the local brew *caju feni* (*fen*, froth) which is strong and potent. Coconut or *palm feni* is made from the sap of the coconut palm. *Feni* is an acquired taste; it is often mixed with soda, salt and lime juice.

Modern Goa

The Goa Legislative Assembly has 40 elected members while the state elects three members to the Lok Sabha, India's central government. Political life is strongly influenced by the regional issue of the relationship with neighbouring Maharashtra. Communal identity also plays a part in elections, with the Congress largely securing the Catholic vote and the BJP winning the support of much of the Hindu population. There is also a strong environmental lobby, in which the Catholic Church plays a role. Goa has had a series of unstable governments with periods of governors imposed by the central government to try and override failures of the democratic process. The state assembly elections in 2007 saw the Congress win 16 and the BJP 14 of the total of 40 seats, and a Congress administration resumed office under the Chief Ministership of Digambar Kamat, who took office on 8 June 2007. The state elects two, not three, members to the Lok Sabha. In the 2009 elections, these were split evenly between the Congress and the BJP.

In common with much of India's west coast, Goa's rural economy depends on rice as the main food crop, cash crops being dominated by coconut, cashew and areca. Mangos, pineapples and bananas are also important. Seasonal water shortages have prompted the development of irrigation projects, the latest of which was the interstate Tillari Project in Pernem *taluka*. Iron ore and bauxite have been two of the state's major exports but heavy industrial development has remained limited to pockets in the east. Tourism (domestic and international) remains one of the state's biggest earners, and money also comes in the form of remittance cheques from overseas workers stationed in the Gulf or working on cruise ships.

Contents

Footnotes

Language

Konkani words and phrases

Travellers in the 'tourist' areas of Goa can quite easily get by without any knowledge of Konkani or Hindi. Learning and using a few local words, as needed, when visiting a foreign country, is always received warmly.

Pronunciation

a̱ as in **ah**
o̱ as in **oh**
u̱ as in **hub**
i̱ as in **bee**
u as oo in **book**

t and d are usually soft (dental) eg di as in **thee**
j is often pronounced like z
Nasalized vowels are shown as an, in, em, etc.
Place names often end with a nasal vowel eg Pern**em**.
NB these marks to help with pronunciation do not appear in the main text.

General

Hello	Hullo
How are you? (m)	Tu̱n kosso assa?
How are you? (f)	Tun kosheam (girl)/ koshi (woman) assi?
My name is...	Mhujem na̱on...
Cheers!	Viva!
Goodbye	Barem!/ Adeus!
Pardon?	Kite-m mhalle-m?
Sorry	Tchuk zali̱
Thankyou	Deo barem korun/obrigad
May I take a photo?	Photo kadum?
Yes/no	Hoi/Na
clean	limp/saf̱
closed	bandh
dirty	sooj
drink	pio-mche-m/pionk
food	khanem
fruit	pho̱ll
cashew	kazu̱

coconut	na̱ll
green coconut	a̱dsaṟ
mango	ambo̱
orange	laranja
pineapple	ananas
good	bare-m
hot (temp)	huṉ
hot (spicy)	tikẖ
shop	du̱kan
water	u̱dak

Health

medicine	awkhad
Please get a doctor	Matso dotorac affoi
I have a fever	Mhaka zor a̱ila
I feel unwell	Haon baro na
I have a stomach ache	Marjay pottan charpta
I have diarrhoea	Maka bhairi zalya

Hotel

I want a room please	Mhaka yek room zai mellat
...with a toilet	Rooman mhaka toilet zai̱
What is the room rate?	Roomachem bhade-m kitte-m?
I'd like to see it	Mhaka room dekhu̱n zai
...larger room	...whodlo̱ room
Please clean the room	Matso room sa̱f kor
There is no hot water/soap	Rooman gorom udak/sabu na̱

Shopping

How much is this?	Yay kitlay poishay?
I'll have this	Haon hemghetan
Too much	Ekdom mharaog
Make it cheaper	Matshemunnay kor
I don't want it	Mhaka naka tem

Travel

I need a taxi	Mhaka taxi zai
Can I share a taxi?	Taxi bhagak korunya?
How much to Colva?	Colwa kitlay podtollay?
Where is the bus station?	Bus station khain assa?
Next bus?	Dusri bus kenna?
How far is Panjim?	Ponnji kithli poiss assa?
How long will it take?	Kithlo wogauth?
I want to hire a cycle	Mhaka yek cycle bhadyak zai

Time and day

now	attants
morning	sakal
afternoon	donpara
evening	sanz

night	rat
at night	ratin
today	az
tomorrow	falya-m
yesterday	kal
Sunday	Ai-tar
Monday	Somar
Tuesday	Mungllar
Wednesday	Budhwar
Thursday	Birestar
Friday	Sukrar
Saturday	Shenwar

Numbers

1	yek
2	don
3	tin
4	char
5	pants
6	so
7	sat
8	atth
9	nnov
10	dha
20	wiss
100	shumber
1000	hazar

Eating out

Eating out in India is normally cheap and safe, but menus can be dauntingly long and full of unfamiliar names. North Indian dishes are nearly universal. Outside their home states, regional dishes are normally only served in specialist restaurants.

Restaurant

Menu please	Matso menu di
Bill please	Matshe-m bill di
I'll have this	Haon hemkhatan
A bottle of water	Udkachi yek batli
No chillies please	Mhaka tikh naka
No ice/sugar please	burf/sakhar naka
Sugar and milk please	Matsi sakhar ani dudh di
Spoon/fork/knife	tchomcho/kantto/souri

Goan dishes

Ambok tik A hot, cour tamarind and chilli curry made with shark, squid or ray and eaten with rice.

Apa de camarão A spicy prawn pie with rice flour crust.

Balchão Prawn, king fish or meat in a red chilli and onion sauce served with bread.

Cafrial Meat marinated in pepper and garlic and braised over a slow fire.

Caldo/Caldinha Delicately spiced light fish and vegetable soup.

Chouriço Goan pork sausage boiled or fried with onions, chillies and feni, often eaten stuffed in bread.

Feijoada Haricot bean (*feijão*) stew; sometimes served with chouriço.

Guisado Tomato-based soup.

Kishmaur Ground, dried shrimp mixed with shredded coconut and chopped onion, served as an accompaniment.

Recheiado Whole fish stuffed with a hot masala sauce.

Seet corri Fish curry with coconut rice.

Sorpotel A highly spiced dish of pickled pig's liver and heart, seasoned with vinegar and tamarind. Perhaps the most famous of Goan meat dishes!

Soupa de carna Spicy soup made with meat and rice stock.

Vindaloo Spicy pork or beef, marinated in garlic, wine vinegar and chillies. Elsewhere in India, *vindaloo* often refers to a hot, spicy curry.

Xacutti 'Shakooti': Hot chicken or meat dish prepared with coconut, pepper and star anise (fr chacontine).

Goan bread

Goan bread is good and there are tasty European-style biscuits.

Kankonn Hard and crispy and shaped like a bangle; often dunked in tea.

Pão Crusty bread rolls, soft inside.

Pollee Like a chapatti; often stuffed with vegetables.

Sannan Goan version of *idli* made with ground rice, coconut and fermented palm *sap* (toddy).

Undo A had crust round bread.

Goan sweets

Sweets are sometimes too sweet for the Western palate.

Alebele A sweet pancake with a coconut filling.

Bebinca A layered coconut pancake and jaggery delicacy made with egg yolks, coconut milk, sugar, nutmeg and ghee.

Doce Fudge-like sweet made with nuts, chickpeas and milk.

Dodol A mix of jaggery and coconut with rice floud/semolina and cashew.

Neuro Semi-circular pastry.

Index